Praise from Job Seekers for the *Knock 'em Dead* Books

"My job search began a few months ago when I found out that I would be laid off because of a corporate buyout. By following your advice, I have had dozens of interviews and have received three very good job offers. Your excellent advice made my job hunt much easier."

—K.C., St. Louis, Missouri

"I've used *Knock 'em Dead* since 1994 when I graduated. It's the reason I've made it to VP—thank you!"

—P.L., Norfolk, Virginia

"My son called me from college last night, desperate to help a friend on her first interview. My advice? Tell her to drop everything and head to the nearest bookstore to get *Knock 'em Dead*. The book is a godsend and helped me obtain the job of my dreams eight years ago. It is by far THE best book on interviewing out there. I highly recommend it to everyone I know who asks me for help. As a Director of HR now, I know. No one should go to an interview without reading, re-reading, and re-re-reading this informative, absorbing, tremendously helpful book. It is utterly amazing. Thank you!"

—S.D., Philadelphia, Pennsylvania

"I was out of work for four months—within five weeks of reading your book, I had four job offers."

—S.K., Dallas, Texas

"I cannot tell you what a fabulous response I have been getting due to the techniques you describe in your books. Besides giving me the tools I needed to 'get my foot in the door,' they gave me confidence. I never thought I could secure an excellent position within a month!"

—B.G., Mountain View, California

"I am very grateful for your *Knock 'em Dead* series. I have read the trio and adopted the methods. In the end, I got a dream job with a salary that is almost double my previous! By adopting your methods, I got four job offers and had a hard time deciding!"

—C.Y., Singapore

"After reading your book, *Knock 'em Dead Resumes*, I rewrote my resume and mailed it to about eight companies. The results were beyond belief. I was employed by one of the companies that got my new resume and received offers of employment or requests for interviews from every company. The entire job search took only five weeks."

—J.V., Dayton, Ohio

"Your book is simply fantastic. This one book improved my yearly income by several thousand dollars, and my future income by untold amounts. Your work has made my family and myself very happy."

—M.Z., St. Clair Shores, Michigan

"After having seen you on television, I decided to order the *Knock 'em Dead* books. Your insights into selling myself helped me find opportunities in my field that would not have been attainable otherwise."

—E. M., Short Hills, New Jersey

"I just wanted to say thank you so much for your book. I can really, honestly say that it has influenced my life course!"

—P.B., London, England

"Thank you for your wonderful book! I read it before attempting to secure a position in an industry that I had been out of for fourteen years. The first company I interviewed with made me an offer for more money than I had expected."

—K.T., Houston, Texas

Praise from Job Seekers for the *Knock 'em Dead* Books

"I got the position! I was interviewed by three people and the third person asked me all the questions in *Knock 'em Dead*. I had all the right answers!"

—D.J., Scottsdale, Arizona

"I followed the advice in *Knock 'em Dead* religiously and got more money, less hours, a better hospital plan, and negotiated to keep my three weeks of vacation. I start my new job immediately!"

—A.B., St. Louis, Missouri

"Thank you for all the wonderfully helpful information you provided in your book. I lost my job almost one year ago. I spent almost eight months looking for a comparable position. Then I had the good sense to buy your book. Two months later, I accepted a new position. You helped me turn one of the worst experiences of my life into a blessing in disguise."

—L.G., Watervliet, New York

"I heard of your book right after I bombed out on three interviews. I read it. I went on two interviews after reading it. I have been told by both of those last two interviewers that I am the strongest candidate. I may have two job offers!"

—B.V., Albuquerque, New Mexico

"I read your book and studied your answers to tough questions. The first interview that I went on after doing this ended up in a job being offered to me! The interviewer told me that I was the best interviewee she'd seen! Thanks a million for writing your book. I am so thankful that I had heard about you!"

—K.P., Houston, Texas

"I just finished writing the letter I have dreamed of writing for three years: my letter of resignation from the Company from Hell. Thanks to you and the book *Knock 'em Dead*, I have been offered and have accepted an excellent position with a major international service corporation."

—C.C., Atlanta, Georgia

"I was sending out hordes of resumes and hardly getting a nibble—and I have top-notch skills and experience in my field. I wasn't prepared for this tough job market. When I read your book, however, I immediately began applying some of your techniques. My few nibbles increased to so many job interviews I could hardly keep up with them!"

—C.S., Chicago, Illinois

"It was as if the interviewer had just put the same book down! After being unemployed for more than a year, I am grateful to say that I've landed the best job I've ever had."

—E.M., Honolulu, Hawaii

"Every time I've used your book, I've gotten an offer! This book is incredible. Thanks for publishing such a great tool."

—W.Z., Columbia, Maryland

"I just received the offer of my dreams with an outstanding company. Thank you for your insight. I was prepared!"

—T.C., San Francisco, California

KnOCK DEaD 'em

COVER LETTERS

12TH EDITION

Cover letters and strategies to get the job you want

MARTIN YATE, CPC

New York Times bestseller

Avon, Massachusetts

To your good fortune, that intersection of preparation, effort, and opportunity

Published by
Adams Media, a division of F+W Media, Inc.
57 Littlefield Street, Avon, MA 02322. U.S.A.
www.adamsmedia.com

ISBN 10: 1-4405-9618-2
ISBN 13: 978-1-4405-9618-6
eISBN 10: 1-5072-0159-1
eISBN 13: 978-1-5072-0159-6

Printed in the United States of America.

10   9   8   7   6   5   4   3   2   1

Library of Congress Cataloging-in-Publication Data
Yate, Martin.
Knock 'em dead cover letters, 12th edition / Martin Yate.
Avon, Massachusetts: Adams Media, 2016.
Includes bibliographical references and index.
LCCN 2016020841 | ISBN 9781440596186 (pb) | ISBN 1440596182 (pb)
LCSH: Cover letters. | Resumes (Employment) | Job hunting.
LCC HF5383 .Y378 2016 | DDC 650.14/2--dc23
LC record available at https://lccn.loc.gov/2016020841

This publication is designed to provide accurate and authoritative information with regard to the subject matter covered. It is sold with the understanding that the publisher is not engaged in rendering legal, accounting, or other professional advice. If legal advice or other expert assistance is required, the services of a competent professional person should be sought.

—From a *Declaration of Principles* jointly adopted by a Committee of the American Bar Association and a Committee of Publishers and Associations

Many of the designations used by manufacturers and sellers to distinguish their products are claimed as trademarks. Where those designations appear in this book and F+W Media, Inc. was aware of a trademark claim, the designations have been printed with initial capital letters.

Cover design by Heather McKiel.

This book is available at quantity discounts for bulk purchases.
For information, please call 1-800-289-0963.

READ THIS FIRST

At every stage of the job search and hiring cycle, letters can help you make important points that can be difficult to express verbally. Use the strategies and tactics I'll show you in this book to position yourself as someone worth taking seriously.

Selling yourself with the written word is a challenge, and probably something you haven't made a priority. However, it is a greatly desired professional skill, and integrating well-crafted letters into your job search can differentiate your candidacy; it's a strategy that can get you out of that dead-end job sooner, or back to work more quickly.

Knock 'em Dead Cover Letters has helped millions of people around the world craft hard-hitting job search letters of all types that helped them land interviews, advance their candidacy, and win job offers, and it can do the same for you.

You'll find job search letters of every conceivable type here: cover letters to headhunters, hiring managers, and more; follow-up letters for after telephone and face-to-face meetings; networking, resurrection, acceptance, and rejection letters; and those jubilant (but mustn't seem so) letters of resignation.

When you write and send a letter, for the recipient, that letter becomes *you*. It speaks for you when you aren't there to speak for yourself; it brings you back and sits you down opposite the recruiter or hiring manager; it keeps you visible and your candidacy vibrant. The letters you send during a job search give your candidacy another dimension: They give you an edge in a competitive job market. The 100-plus sample letters in this book are *real* letters that have already worked in someone's job search. I've helped people write some of these letters, while others have been sent to me by career coaches, headhunters, hiring managers, and grateful readers (I'd very much like to see yours).

EMAIL AND TRADITIONAL MAIL
Throughout this book, the words "mail," "letter," and "email" are intended to be interchangeable, unless otherwise noted. Written communications can be delivered by either email or traditional mail, with the majority of us using email for most communications today. However, you shouldn't ignore traditional mail, because when you do something other job hunters aren't doing, you stand out.

As no one gets much traditional mail anymore, when you follow my directions and identify recruiters and hiring managers by name, you can send your resume by email, and by traditional mail as well: Your envelope will stand out and offer a break from the computer screen.

I know this sounds crazy so let me give you an example. I gave this advice to a client from Microsoft. He objected that he was with a leading tech company and would look foolish sending traditional letters. Then he sighed and said, "Well you seem to know how things work, so I'll give it a shot." On a Thursday he sent out five letters; by the following Wednesday he had received three calls in response. On Wall Street they call going against general consensus "contrarian thinking," and when, like this, it is based on sound thinking the results are often remarkable . . . Oh, and one of those calls led directly to his next job.

When you integrate this clever little tactic into the four-approach plan of attack you learn in *Knock 'em Dead*, it can quadruple the number of your job interviews.

Also effective when sending your resume to someone by email, is to also attach the cover letter as a second document with your resume. This means that when the resume is circulated physically, the cover letter is more likely to go with it. One note of caution: *Never* put a cover letter followed by your resume into one document. It doesn't work; the letter may get read but the resume very often gets overlooked. If you try this, be sure to attach two separate documents.

When You *Must* Use Traditional Mail

There is one type of job search letter that you will always want to format and print out as a traditional letter: your resignation letter. These letters are important because your career is likely to span fifty-plus years, and you have no idea whom you will meet again and under what circumstances. Thus in leaving a company you always want it to be on good terms.

Resigning by email will be seen as insulting and unprofessional. A resignation really has to be done in person, and you'll find that using a printed resignation letter can help ease an always-difficult situation. Here's how you do it with the most finesse and least awkwardness:

1. Have the resignation letter typed and in an envelope.
2. Ask for a meeting. This may happen immediately, so always have the letter ready before making the meeting request. Walk into the manager's office, sit down, and say, " I need to give you this." Offer the letter and sit quietly while your manager reads it. The letter does all the difficult work with words you'd likely never be able to get out in such a stressful situation.

There is a section with well-worded resignation letters later in the book. When worded along the suggested lines, the conversation that follows should be smooth and focused on the transition. The result is that you avoid coming across as angry or a bumbling idiot. Instead you are seen as a poised professional doing things the right way—and as you don't know when you'll meet again, leaving a good impression is always the smart move.

How Recruitment Works

A good cover letter and subsequent follow-up letters can speed your candidacy through the four stages all employers go through in the recruitment, screening, and selection cycle. They won't win you the job in and of themselves, but they can make a big difference in the way you are perceived, helping you stand out from the competition. The four stages are:

1. *Long list development.* Multiple recruitment strategies to develop the largest manageable field of qualified candidates, usually ten to twelve.
2. *Short-list development.* The long list of candidates is screened for best-fit-to-the-job, reducing the long list to four to six candidates. Those who make the cut become the "short list," and are invited in for an interview, after first passing the additional screening of a telephone interview. A folder is created for each candidate, including both print and electronic docs.
3. *Short-list prioritization.* Through a series of interviews, usually one, two, or three, the short-list candidates are ranked for ability and fit.
4. *Short-list review and decision.* Each candidate's folder is reviewed one last time before the final decision. The folder will include your resume, the employer's notes, and any cover and follow-up letters you have been smart enough to send during the interview process. These letters make additional points, clear up mistakes and omissions, and serve to brand you as a competent professional.

ACKNOWLEDGMENTS

Knock 'em Dead books have been in print here in America and in many languages around the world for thirty years and owe their success to constant updating and the millions of satisfied professionals whose careers are helped by them. This is only possible because *Knock 'em Dead* books work; they help you change the trajectory of your professional life.

There is a very small group who helps me write such books, and constantly update classics like *Knock 'em Dead Cover Letters*: Peter Archer, my managing editor; Jane Hauptman, my conscientious copyeditor; and Angela Yate, who takes care of our business and allows me the time to do good work; she also acts as the first sounding board on the many issues that can make the difference between a good book and a perennial classic.

CONTENTS

CHAPTER 8:
Use Cover Letters to Get Four Times the Interviews ... 91
Making the direct approach: how to find the names, titles, and contact information for the people most likely to be able to make you a job offer.

CHAPTER 9:
Sending Out Cover Letters ... 105
How to organize yourself for success.

CHAPTER 10:
Sample Letters ... 109

Chapter 1
Cover Letters: The Secret Weapon of Your Job Search

A recent survey of 1,000 executives revealed that 91 percent found cover letters to be valuable in their evaluation of candidates. Your cover letter can add information that isn't in your resume and help establish a communication channel between two professionals with a common interest.

Cover letters are most effective when you develop a plan of attack that includes reaching out directly to hiring authorities. Whenever someone in a position to hire you reads your resume and cover letter, the odds of getting that interview increase dramatically, because you have skipped right over the initial hurdle—getting pulled from the resume database—and you are pitching directly to a recruiter or hiring manager.

The primary goal of every job search is to *get into conversation, as quickly and as frequently as possible, with people in a position to hire you*, because without conversations, job offers don't get made. Difficulty reaching hiring authorities with the candidate's message is one of the major reasons job searches stall. This happens when job searches involve themselves, almost exclusively, with posting resumes to resume banks and responding to job postings by uploading resumes into other resume databases.

However, when you can get your resume, personalized with a cover letter, in front of recruiters and hiring authorities, you differentiate yourself and dramatically increase your chances of landing an interview.

Recruiters and hiring managers overwhelmingly appreciate cover and follow-up letters. If all you are planning to do is load your resume into resume databases, a cover letter can help, but its main strength is in personalizing your message to a specific company and ideally a specific person. When you develop a plan of attack for your job search that includes reaching out directly to decision-makers, the personalizing touch of a letter really increases your bang.

WHO TO TARGET IN YOUR JOB SEARCH
The hiring titles to target during your job search are:

- Those titles mostly likely to be in a position to hire you. Usually this will be managers 1–3 levels above your target job.
- Those titles most likely to be involved in the selection process. Typically, this will be a manager working in a related department.

Your ideal target for direct communication is always someone who can hire you, although any management title offers opportunity for referral. Even HR contacts are valuable: They can't make the hiring decision, but the pivotal nature of their jobs means HR professionals are aware of all areas within a company that could use your skills.

Any name and title you capture in a job search is valuable. With the Internet at your fingertips, there are countless ways to identify the names of people who hold the titles you need to reach, and if a name and title is of no use to you, hold on to it anyway: It might be just the contact another job hunter needs, so it can be a valuable commodity to leverage in your networking activities. Refer to Chapter 8 for much more information on how to find the names of hiring authorities. For more on leveraging your network and general networking strategies, see the latest edition of *Knock 'em Dead: The Ultimate Job Search Guide*.

When an email or envelope is opened, your cover letter will be the first thing looked at. It personalizes your candidacy for a specific job in ways that are impossible for your resume to do, given its formal nature and structure. The cover letter sets the stage for the reader to accept your resume, and therefore you, as something and someone special. It can create common ground between you and the reader, and demonstrates that you are well qualified and suitable for *this* job with *this* company.

Cover Letter Tactics

Address Your Target by Name

Your first step is to grab the reader's attention and arouse interest, so whenever possible address the letter to someone by name.

Approaching recruiters and hiring authorities directly is one of the very best tactics for getting job offers. Whenever you can find the names of any one of these titles involved in the recruitment and selection cycle, approach them directly and address them by name. Again, see Chapter 8 for much more information on this topic.

Make Your Letter Readable

Your customer, the reader, is always going to be distracted, so your letters need to be easily readable, focused, clear, and brief. *Your letters should cut to the chase and be both friendly and respectful; they should never be unfocused, pompous, or sound like you swallowed a dictionary.*

You can also grab the reader's attention with the appearance of your letter, which should mirror the fonts and font sizes of your resume, giving you a coordinated and professional look.

Hardly anyone in a position to hire you is still young enough to comfortably read 10-point fonts. Anyone who has been staring at computer screens for ten or more years and has a dozen other priorities pressing for her attention is likely to have problems with tiny font sizes and elaborate but unreadable fonts. I recommend a minimum of 11- or 12-point font size. Applying these rules of matching font and font size to *email and print* letters is easy to do and easily overlooked; but paying attention to the details pays dividends in a job search.

Establish Connectivity

The focus of a cover letter is not "me." Rather it is about "your needs and how I can fulfill them." So the first paragraph should focus on the employer's needs and how you can deliver on those requirements, using language that speaks to the job from the employer's POV. For example, you might say:

You are looking for a B-B sales professional used to dealing with sophisticated corporate clients buying performance technology tools. This would ideally require experience with the pre- and post-sales process for enterprise software, and an educated professional with good social graces who, most importantly, can consistently exceed new sales quota while nurturing and upselling to a growing customer base. This describes me perfectly.

Emphasize Your Personal Brand

Branding is the process by which you consistently draw attention to the bundle of skills and behaviors that make you a little different. All the job search letters you send—and yes, that includes every email—are part of the packaging that captures the *professional you*. If your written words look good and carry a succinct, relevant, readily accessible message that shows you to be a down-to-earth professional with a clear sense of self, you're well on the road to establishing a viable *professional brand*. When your actions differentiate you from others, your standing as a candidate is improved.

What makes you special?

- Just being smart enough to get your resume directly under the nose of a manager, who wants to make a good hire and get back to work, makes you special.
- Getting your resume to the hiring manager in a creative way and showing that you know what you are doing makes you special. Your letter might say in part, "I sent my resume by email, but thought you might appreciate a screen break, so you'll find a hard copy attached to this letter . . ." Your email might note, "As well as attaching my resume to this email, in case you need a screen break, I've also sent it by traditional mail."
- Writing a strong cover letter that presents your resume and establishes connectivity between you and the manager makes you special.
- Keeping your message clear and succinct makes you special.
- Following up your meetings with thoughtful letters that continue the messaging of a consummate professional makes you special and confirms your professional brand.
- Making sure in all your emails and print letters that the fonts are legible and coordinated with your resume makes you special.

Continuity in Written Communication

To ensure continuity in your written communications, make a commitment to:

1. Make the font you employ for contact information and headlines in both your resume and your cover letter the same.
2. Use the same font you chose for your resume's body copy for the message in your cover letter.
3. Use the same font choices for all your email communications. Smart idea: set the chosen font as your default email font.
4. Make the font choices of your written communications consistent with the font choices you employ in email and other electronic communications.

5. Get matching paper for resume, cover letters, and envelopes. Every office superstore has them. Sending your cover letter and resume by traditional mail when the opportunity arises is a great way to get your resume read, because most job hunters don't think to do this. Today, hiring managers get far fewer resumes by mail, but a busy manager still likes a break from the computer screen, so more time is spent reviewing your resume. You'll also need printed resumes to take to interviews.

Cut to the Chase and Stay On-Message

A good cover letter gets your resume read with serious consideration. Time is precious, which means recruiters and hiring authorities won't waste it on a letter that wanders. Your letters should always reflect a professional whose resume will have something to say.

When you can, make a specific reference to a job's key requirements. You want the reader to move from your letter to the resume already thinking, "Here's a candidate who can do the job." You can do this in either of two ways:

- Referencing a job's most important requirements.
- Referencing the issues behind the job's most important requirements.

If an advertisement, a job posting, or a telephone conversation with a potential employer reveals an aspect of a particular job opening that is not addressed in your resume (and for some reason you haven't had time to update it), use a cover letter to fill in the gaps; the Executive Briefing (you'll see samples shortly) is an especially useful tool for this job.

Brevity is important. The letter doesn't sell everything about you; it positions you for serious consideration, hoping to demonstrate that you grasp what is at the heart of the job's deliverables. Leave your reader wanting more.

End with a Call to Action

Just as you work to create a strong opening, make sure your closing carries the same conviction. It is the reader's last personal impression of you, so make it strong, make it tight, and make it obvious that you are serious about entering into meaningful conversation. Your letters should always include a call to action. Explain when, where, and how you can be contacted. You can also be proactive, telling the reader that you intend to follow up at a certain time if he or she has not already contacted you.

Every step of the job search and selection cycle offers opportunities to use letters to leverage your candidacy. A good, strong letter will get your foot in the door, differentiate you from other contenders, and ultimately help you define a distinctive *professional brand*. Although the majority of your communications will be emails, stand out by sending really important information in both emails and traditional letters. If nothing more, by delivering your message through two media, it gets read twice, which increases the odds of your candidacy being noticed and advanced.

Chapter 2
SIX HIGH-MILEAGE COVER LETTERS

Corporate America's wholesale adoption of the Internet as the primary recruitment vehicle has completely changed the way you need to approach your job search.

Every year, the number of resumes loaded into commercial resume databases grows exponentially. Currently, the larger databases each house more than 40 million resumes. Many individual corporate resume banks have more than 1 million resumes stored and social networking sites like LinkedIn have more than 100 million resumes and professional profiles registered. This has made life easier for recruiters, since they can usually find enough qualified candidates in the top twenty resumes from any given database, *and given the large number of potential candidates, they rarely dig deeper.*

In resume databases that allow attachments to your resume, a cover letter helps you stand out by making additional and supportive comments about your capabilities. When you send your resume directly to a recruiter or potential hiring authority by using their name and title, your resume and cover letter have even greater impact because you can differentiate yourself by addressing the hiring manager or recruiter by name and by customizing your message; and most important, you sidestepped the resume databases entirely.

Here are six types of cover letters that can help your job search momentum. Each is a composite letter I built from scouring the examples that appear later in the book, taking a word from one example and a phrase from another. In each example, I have underlined the borrowed phrases to give you an idea of how easy it is to create your own original documents with a little cutting and pasting.

The six letters are:

1. The cover letter for when you do not know of a specific job, but have a name to send the letter to, or are uploading to a resume bank where you can attach your cover letter to your resume
2. The executive briefing. Always effective when you have knowledge of the job's requirements and especially so when you can address someone by name
3. A cover letter in response to an online job posting
4. A cover letter aimed at headhunters
5. A networking letter for getting the word out to the professional community about your search
6. A broadcast letter if your resume doesn't quite fit the job

A Cover Letter When You Do Not Know of a Specific Job Opening

This letter is designed to be uploaded to a database as an attachment or sent to a potential hiring manager whose name you've garnered from your research. Of course, if you are sending this letter to an individual, it should be personalized with a salutation and include references to the company, some detail of the job, or the establishment of common ground between you and the recipient.

James Sharpe
18 Central Park Street • Anytown, NY 14788
(516) 555-1212

October 2, 20—

Jackson Bethell, V.P. Operations
DataLink Products
621 Miller Drive
Anytown, CA 91234

Dear Jackson Bethell:

Recently I have been researching the leading local companies in data communications. My search has been for companies that are respected in the field and that provide ongoing training programs. The name of DataLink Products keeps coming up as a top company.

I am an experienced voice and data communications specialist with a substantial background in IBM environments. If you have an opening for someone in this area, you will see that my resume demonstrates a person of unusual dedication, efficiency, and drive. My experience and achievements include:

- The complete redesign of a data communications network, projected to increase efficiency company-wide by some 12 percent.
- The installation and troubleshooting of a Defender IV callback security system for a dial-up network.

I enclose a copy of my resume, and look forward to examining any of the ways you feel my background and skills would benefit DataLink Products. While I prefer not to use my employer's time taking personal calls at work, with discretion I can be reached at (516) 555-1212 to initiate contact. However, I would rather you call me at _____ in the evening. Let's talk!

Yours truly,

James Sharpe

James Sharpe

JAF A SOAB L

18 Central Park Street, Anytown, NY 14788

(516) 555-1212

David Doors, Director of Marketing   January 14, 20—
Martin Financial Group
1642 Rhode Island Way
Anytown, NY 01234

Dear David Doors:

I have always followed the performance of your company in *Mutual Funds Newsletter*.

Recently your notice regarding a Market Analyst in *Investor's Business Daily* caught my eye—and your company name caught my attention. Your record over the last three years shows exceptional portfolio management. Because of my experience with one of your competitors, I know I could make significant contributions.

I would like to talk to you about your personnel needs and how I am able to contribute to your department's goals.

An experienced market analyst, I have an economics background (M.S. Purdue) and a strong quantitative analysis approach to market fluctuations. This combination has enabled me to consistently pick the new technology flotations that are the backbone of the growth-oriented mutual fund. For example:

I first recommended Targus Fund six years ago. More recently my clients have been strongly invested in Atlantic Horizon Growth (in the high-risk category), and Next Wave Growth and Income (for the cautious investor). Those following my advice over the last six years have consistently outperformed the market.

I know that resumes help you sort out the probables from the possibles, but they are no way to judge the personal caliber of an individual. I would like to meet with you and demonstrate that along with the credentials, I have the professional commitment that makes for a successful team player.

Yours truly,

Jane Swift

Jane Swift

The Executive Briefing

The executive briefing is an effective form of cover letter to use *whenever you have information about a job opening*—perhaps from an online job posting, a lead, or a conversation with one of your network contacts—*and there is a good skill match*. The executive briefing gets right to the point and makes life easy for the reader. It introduces your resume, as well as customizing and supplementing it. Why is an executive briefing so effective?

1. It quickly matches job requirements against the skills you bring to the table, making analysis much easier for the reader and a successful outcome more likely for you.
2. Since an initial screener (someone who quickly sorts through cover letters and resumes to separate the wheat from the chaff) may not have an in-depth understanding of the job's requirements, the executive briefing simplifies things by matching the job's requirements point by point to your abilities.
3. The executive briefing allows you to emphasize your skills in a particular area or fill any gaps in your resume with job-specific information.
4. If an opportunity comes along that is a slam dunk for you, but your resume isn't current or doesn't have the right focus, the executive briefing allows you to update your work history. This very professional quick fix is a godsend when someone asks to see your resume but it isn't up-to-date.

From: top10acct@aol.com
Subject: Re: Accounting Manager
Date: February 18, 2005 10:05:44 PM EST
To: rlstein@McCoy.com

Dear Ms. Stein:

I have nine years of accounting experience and am responding to your recent posting for an Accounting Manager on CareerBuilder. Please allow me to highlight my skills as they relate to your stated requirements.

Your Requirements	**My Experience**
Accounting degree, 4 years exp.	Obtained a C.A. degree in 2000 and have over four years' experience as an Accounting Manager
Excellent people skills and leadership	Effectively managed a staff of 24; ability to motivate staff, including supervisors
Strong administrative skills	Assisted in the development of a base reference skills–library with Microsoft Excel for 400 clients
Good communication skills	Trained new supervisors and staff via daily coaching sessions, communication meetings, and technical skills sessions

My resume, pasted below and attached in MSWord, will flesh out my general background. I hope this executive briefing helps you use your time effectively today. I am ready to make a move. I hope we can talk soon.

Sincerely,

Joe Black
Joe Black

The executive briefing assures that each resume you send out addresses the job's specific needs. It provides a comprehensive picture of a thorough professional, plus a personalized, fast, and easy-to-read synopsis that details exactly how your background matches the job description.

A Cover Letter in Response to an Online Job Posting

If you are writing in response to an online job posting, you should mention both the website and any reference codes associated with the job:

"I read your job posting on your company's website on January 5th and felt I had to respond . . ."

"Your online job posting regarding a _____ on _____ .com caught my eye, and your company name caught my attention."

"This email, and my attached resume, is in response to job posting #145 on _____ ."

Email in Response to an Online Job Posting

From: Helen Darvik [darviklegalpro@earthlink.net]
To: ggoodfellow@budownoble.com
Cc:
Subject: Administrator/mgmnt/mktg/cmptr/acctg/planning/personnel

Dear Ms. _____:

I am responding to your job posting on HotJobs.com for a legal administrator of a law firm. I wrote to you on (date) about law administrator positions in the metropolitan _____ area. I have attached another resume of my educational background and employment history. I am very interested in this position.

I have been a legal administrator for two twenty-one-attorney law firms during the past six years. In addition, I have been a law firm consultant for over a year. Besides my law firm experience, I have been a medical administrator for over ten years. I believe that all of this experience will enable me to manage the law firm in this position very successfully. I possess the management, marketing, computer, accounting/budgeting, financial-planning, personnel, and people-oriented skills that will have a very positive impact on this law firm.

I will be in the _____ area later in the month, so hopefully, we can meet at that time to discuss this position. I look forward to hearing from you, Ms. _____, concerning this position. Thank you for your time and consideration.

Very truly yours,

Helen Darvik
(516) 555-1212
darviklegalpro@earthlink.net

A Cover Letter to a Headhunter

Headhunters deserve your respect. They are, after all, the most sophisticated sales-people in the world—they sell products that talk back. A headhunter will be only faintly amused by your exhortations "to accept the challenge" or "test your skills by finding me a job" in the brief moment before he practices hoops with your letter and the trash can.

When approaching and working with headhunters—whether they are working for the local employment agency, a contingency, or a retained search firm—bear in mind these two rules and you won't go far wrong:

1. Tell the truth. Answer questions truthfully and you will likely receive help. Get caught in a lie and you will have established a career-long environment of distrust with someone who probably possesses a very diverse and influential list of contacts.
2. Cut immediately to the chase in your letters and conversations. For example:

"I am forwarding my resume, because I understand you specialize in representing employers in the _____ field."

"Please find the enclosed resume. As a specialist in the _____ field, I felt you might be interested in the skills of a _____."

"Among your many clients there may be one or two who are seeking an experienced professional for a position as a _____."

Remember that in a cover letter sent to executive search firms and employment agencies, you should mention your salary and, if appropriate, your geographic considerations. If you want to work with headhunters productively, read the latest edition of *Knock 'em Dead: The Ultimate Job Search Guide.*

Here is an example of a cover letter you might send to a corporate headhunter:

Letter to a Headhunter

James Sharpe
18 Central Park Street • Anytown, NY 14788
(516) 555-1212

December 2, 20—

Dear Mr. O'Flynn:

I am forwarding my resume, as I understand that you specialize in the accounting profession. As you may be aware, the management structure at _____ will be reorganized in the near future. While I am enthusiastic about the future of the agency under its new leadership, I have elected to make this an opportunity for change and professional growth.

My many years of experience lend themselves to a finance management position in any medium-sized service firm, but I am open to other opportunities. Although I would prefer to remain in New York, I would entertain other areas of the country, if the opportunity warrants it. I am currently earning $65,000 a year.

I have enclosed my resume for your review. Should you be conducting a search for someone with my background at the present time or in the near future, I would greatly appreciate your consideration. I would be happy to discuss my background more fully with you on the phone or in a personal interview.

Very truly yours,

James Sharpe

James Sharpe

JS
Resume attached

Networking Letters

Nothing works like a personal recommendation from a fellow professional. It is no accident that successful people in all fields either know each other or at least know *of* each other. You get the most out of networking by being connected to your profession and the professionals within it. Networking is a topic beyond the scope of this book, so you'll want to check out networking strategies in the latest edition of *Knock 'em Dead: The Ultimate Job Search Guide.*

Here are important considerations to bear in mind with networking letters:

1. Establish connectivity. Recall the last memorable contact you had with the person, or mention someone that you have both spoken to recently. Use common past employers, membership in professional associations, interests, or a topical event as a bridge builder.

    If you are writing (and calling) as the result of a referral, say so and quote the person's name if appropriate:

    "I am writing because our mutual colleague, John Stanovich, felt my skills and abilities would be valuable to your company . . ."

    "The manager of your San Francisco branch, Pamela Bronson, suggested I contact you regarding the opening for a _____."

    "I received your name last week from Henry Charles, the branch manager of Savannah Bank, and he suggested I contact you. In case the resume he forwarded is caught up in the mail, I enclosed another."

    "Arthur Gold, your office manager and my neighbor, thought I should contact you about the upcoming opening in your accounting department."

2. Tell them why you are writing:

    "It's time for me to make a move; my job just got sent to Mumbai, India, and I'm hoping you could help me with a new sense of direction."

3. Do not talk about your ideal job. This only narrows the opportunities people will tell you about. Instead, just let contacts know your qualifications/experience and the job title you are most likely to work under. Don't let ego cost you a valuable job lead.

4. Ask for advice and guidance:

   "What do you think are the growing companies in our industry today?"

   "Could you take a look at my resume for me? I really need an objective opinion and I've always respected your viewpoint."

5. Never ask directly, " Do you have a job opening?", "Can you hire me?", or "Can your company hire me?" Instead, ask to talk on the telephone for a few minutes. Then by all means ask for leads within specific target companies.

6. When you do get help, say thank you. If you get the help in conversation, follow it up in writing: The impression is indelible and it just might get you another lead.

Networking Letter (Computer and Information Systems Manager)

This letter was sent to follow up a meeting with a medical school dean

DAVID KENT

1623 St. Louis Way • Honolulu, Hawaii 96813

808-555-6256 • dkent@alohanet.com

January 14, 20–

John Jones, M.D.
Dean, School of Medicine
University of Hawaii
1234 East-West Circle
Honolulu, Hawaii 96822

Dear Dr. Jones:

Perhaps you remember our chance meeting at the Bio Asia-Pacific Conference at the Sheraton Waikiki on August 18 and 19, 20–. In our brief conversation, I shared with you the idea of utilizing Web Development as an administrative tool. You expressed interest in the possibility of implementing such a system within the School of Medicine.

May I suggest a formal meeting to explore the idea?

I have some exciting and creative ideas, which may encourage you to take the next step toward realizing the positive impact a content management system would have in the School of Medicine. This would also be a great opportunity for us to discuss your goals and how an administrative intranet would help you reach them in a more timely and cost-effective manner.

In addition, there has recently been spirited discussion within the IT community on the topic of organizational continuity and its potential vulnerability due to advances in technology. I think you'll find the specific strategies I have to share with you worthy of consideration.

If you recall, my background is in Web Planning and Development, with specific skills in developing administrative intranets and public websites, and designing web-based software to address the internal and external reporting needs of organizations.

Enclosed is my resume attesting to my experience and specialties. I will contact you within the next few days to discuss the possibility of meeting with you.

Respectfully,
David Kent
Computer and Information Systems Manager

Enclosure: Resume

The Broadcast Letter

The broadcast letter acts as a brief introduction of the skills you bring to the table and is designed to be sent without a resume. You can use it when:

- You don't have a relevant resume.
- Your resume is inappropriate for the position.
- Your resume isn't getting the results you want, and you want to try something different while you are retooling it.

To be effective, the information you use in a broadcast letter must speak directly to the specific needs of a job posting or be focused on the needs of this job as you have determined them from your resume's Target Job Deconstruction exercises (more on this shortly). This is because the intent of the broadcast letter is to *replace* the resume as a means of introduction and to initiate conversation. Keep in mind that although a broadcast letter can get you into a telephone conversation with a potential employer, that employer is still likely to ask for a resume.

While I am not a big fan of broadcast letters, people have used them effectively, so you need to be aware of them. As they pretty much require you have a name to send them to, my feeling is that, as a resume is going to be requested anyway, you should take the time to customize your resume properly. I don't advise using this kind of letter as the spearhead or sole thrust of your campaign, but you can use it as a stopgap measure when you are retooling an ineffective resume or are otherwise regrouping.

Broadcast Letter

JAF A SOAB L
18 Central Park Street, Anytown, NY 14788
(516) 555-1212

October 2, 20—

Dear _____ :

For the past seven years I have pursued an increasingly successful career in the sales profession. Among my accomplishments I include:

SALES
As a regional representative, I contributed $1,500,000, or 16 percent, of my company's annual sales. I am driven by achievement.

MARKETING
My marketing skills (based on a B.S. in marketing) enabled me to increase sales 25 percent in my economically stressed territory, at a time when colleagues were striving to maintain flat sales. Repeat business reached an all-time high. I am persistent and pay attention to detail.

PROJECT MANAGEMENT
Following the above successes, my regional model was adopted by the company. I trained and provided project supervision to the entire sales force. The following year, company sales showed a sales increase 12 percent above projections. I am a committed team player, motivated by the group's overall success.

The above was based on my firmly held zero price–discounting philosophy. I don't cut margins to make a sale. It is difficult to summarize my work in a letter. The only way I can imagine providing you the opportunity to examine my credentials is for us to talk with each other. I look forward to hearing from you. Please call me at _____ .

Yours sincerely,

Jane Swift
Jane Swift

Chapter 3

KNOW THE JOB, KNOW YOUR CUSTOMER

Think of potential employers like your customers. If you listen to what your customers are saying, you will find that they will tell you exactly what they want to "buy." Understanding what is important to your customer (the employer) helps you understand what that customer wants to buy and what you need to sell.

If you work in sales, marketing, marketing communications, or are in any way close to bringing in revenue for your employer, you will understand the importance of "getting inside your customers' heads" to find out what is important to them, because this allows you to sell the product or service based on the customers' needs. Knowing what customers want to buy makes it much easier to customize your message to meet their needs.

All the insights you need to write a good cover letter are already available to you in job postings. *All you need to do is learn how to translate them into usable information*, which is what we are going to do now.

What follows is a simple exercise called Target Job Deconstruction (TJD). *Do not skip this exercise: It can make an enormous difference to this job search and to your entire future career development.* It will tell you precisely how to prioritize the information you offer employers, and will give you examples for your letters and a new way of understanding what it is you actually get paid for. The exercise will also tell you the topics you're most likely to be asked about at interviews, and prepare you with suggestions for answers to those questions.

This exercise is geared toward:

- Determining the precise requirements of the job you want
- Matching your skill set to those requirements
- Identifying the story you need to tell in your cover letter and resume to highlight the match between your skills and those requirements

The Target Job Deconstruction

The most difficult part of any letter is knowing what to say and how to say it, but the TJD approach ensures that the topics your letter addresses are going to be of the greatest interest to your customers, and the words you use will have the greatest likelihood of resonating with the reader.

Step One

Collect six job postings for the job you are best qualified to do, and save them in a folder. Try to use jobs located in your target area, but if you don't have enough local jobs, collect job descriptions from anywhere. For Target Job Deconstruction, the location of the job doesn't matter; what's important is understanding how employers *define*, *prioritize*, and *express* their needs.

Step Two

Open a new Microsoft Word document and title it TJD for *Target Job Deconstruction*. Add a subhead reading *Job Title*, then copy and paste in the variations from each of your sample job descriptions. Looking at the result, you can say, "When employers are hiring people like *me*, they tend to describe the job title with these words."

From these examples, you then come up with a *Target Job Title* for your resume. You'll add this line right after your name and contact information. These words help your resume perform well in resume database searches and act as a headline, giving human eyes an immediate focus on who and what the resume is about. This again helps your resume's performance.

Step Three

Add a second subhead titled: *Skills/Responsibilities/Experience/Deliverables*.

Look through the job postings for a *single requirement* that's common to all six of your job postings. Take the most complete description of that *single requirement* and copy and paste it into your TJD document, putting a "6" by your entry to signify that it is common to all of them.

Check the other job postings for different words and phrases used to describe this same job skill, and copy and paste them beneath the entry you created. Repeat this exercise for other requirements common to all six of your sample job postings. The result will be a list of the skills/requirements that all employers feel are of prime importance, and the words they use to describe them.

Step Four

Repeat this process for requirements common to five of the jobs, and then four, and so on all the way down to those requirements mentioned in only one job posting.

When this is done, you can look at your work and say, "When employers are hiring people like *me*, they tend to refer to them by these job titles; they prioritize their needs in *this* way, and use *these* words to describe their prioritized needs." At this point you have a template for the story your resume needs to tell.

Step Five

Generate illustrative examples of your competency with the skills that employers identify as priorities. You should remember that jobs are only ever added to the payroll for two reasons:

1. To make money or save money for the company, or to otherwise increase productivity.
2. To identify, prevent, and solve the problems/challenges that occur in your area of expertise and that interfere with the company's pursuit of (1).

Working through your list of prioritized employer requirements, identify the problems that typically arise when you are executing your duties in that particular area of the job. Then for each problem identify:

- How do you execute your responsibilities to prevent this problem from arising in the first place?
- How do you tackle such a situation when it does occur? Think of specific examples.
- Whenever you can, quantify the results of your actions in terms of productivity increase, money earned, or money saved.

Step Six

Going back to the prioritized requirements you identified in earlier steps, consider each individual requirement and recall the **best** person you have ever known doing that aspect of the job. Next, identify what made that person stand out in your mind as a true professional; think of personality, skills, and behaviors. Perhaps she always had a smile, listened well, and had good critical thinking and time-management skills.

Together with the specific technical skills of the job you have already identified, the traits of the person who stands out in your mind will give you a *behavioral profile of the person every employer wants to hire*, plus a behavioral blueprint for subsequent professional success.

Step Seven

Looking one last time at the list of prioritized requirements in your TJD, consider each individual requirement and recall the **worst** person you have ever known doing that aspect of the job. Perhaps he was passive-aggressive, never listened, and was rarely on time with projects or for meetings.

This time you will have a complete *behavioral profile of the person no employer wants to hire* and a behavioral blueprint for professional failure.

Pulling It All Together

Target Job Deconstruction will give you the insight into your target job to maximize your resume's productivity both in resume databases and with recruiters and hiring managers. The process also uncovers the areas of the job that will hold specific interest for a hiring manager and therefore likely give rise to interview questions. And because you have thought things through, you will now have answers to those questions and will be able to illustrate them with examples.

Last, but by no means least, you also have a behavioral blueprint for professional success: no small thing to possess.

GET A FREE RESUME REVIEW FROM MARTIN YATE!
Go to the website of the store where you bought the book, write an honest review, and send the link with your resume to *MartinYate@KnockEmDead.com*.

Chapter 4
How to Identify and Build a Desirable Professional Brand

A resume is the primary tool that all professionals use to define and disseminate their *professional brand* to an ever-expanding world of contacts. Long-term success—rewarding work (without layoffs) and professional growth that fits your goals—is much easier to achieve when you are credible and visible within your profession. Creating and nurturing a *professional brand* as part of your overall career-management strategy will help you build credibility and visibility throughout your profession, because an identifiable brand gives you focus and motivation, and gives others a way to differentiate you.

Establishing a desirable *professional brand* takes time; after all, you have to brand something that is worth branding, something with which your customers will resonate. It is something that evolves over years, but you need to start somewhere and you need to start now.

The greater the effort you put into working toward credibility and visibility, which over time translates into a steadily growing professional reputation in your area of expertise, the quicker you enter the inner circles in your department, your company, and ultimately your profession. And it is in these inner circles that job security, plum assignments, raises, promotions, and professional marketability all dwell.

Think of your brand as the formal announcement to the professional community of how you want to be seen in your professional world. Your resume and an accompanying cover letter will be the primary tools you will use to deliver this focused and consistent message of your brand. It's the narrative of your resume, and the complementary themes echoed in all your job search letters, that tell this story in a very particular way: by capturing your experience, skills, capabilities, and professional behavioral profile *as they relate to what your customers want to buy.*

Components of a Desirable Professional Brand

A viable *professional brand* must be built on firm foundations. This means you must understand what employers want and look for when they hire (and subsequently promote) someone in your profession, at your level, and with your job title. Reaching this level of understanding of how your employers think is critical for the success of this job search and for your career going forward; it's why you spent Chapter Three learning how employers think about your work, and how they prioritize and express those thoughts . . . and by extension how they will reward those who give them what they want.

In this chapter, you'll examine some additional and equally important dimensions of the *professional you*; dimensions that will play into your resume, your interviews, and your success in that next step on your career path. Specifically, we'll examine something called *transferable skills*, and see how they can be used in your cover and other job search letters.

Transferable Skills and Professional Values

Over the years I've read a lot a lot of books about finding jobs, winning promotions, and managing your career. A few were insightful and many were innocuous, but one theme that runs through them all is the absurd and harmful advice to, "Just be yourself."

"Who you are is just fine. Be yourself and you'll do fine." Wrong. Remember that first day on your first job, when you went to get your first cup of coffee? You found the coffee machine, and there, stuck on the wall behind it, was a handwritten sign reading:

YOUR MOTHER DOESN'T WORK HERE
PICK UP AFTER YOURSELF

You thought, "Pick up after myself? Gee, that means I can't behave like I do at home and get away with it." And so you started to observe and emulate the more successful professionals around you. You behaved in a way that was appropriate to the environment, and in doing so demonstrated *emotional intelligence*. Over time you developed many new ways of conducting yourself at work in order to be accepted as a professional in your field. You weren't born this way. You developed a behavioral profile, a *professional persona* that enabled you to survive in the professional world.

Some people are just better than the average bear at everything they do, and they become more successful as a result. It doesn't happen by accident; there is a specific set of *transferable skills* and *professional values* that underlies professional success: skills and values that employers all over the world in every industry and profession are anxious to find in candidates from the entry level to the boardroom. Why this isn't taught in schools and in the university programs that cost a small fortune is unfathomable, because these skills and values are the foundation of every successful career. They break down into these groups:

1. *The Technical Skills of Your Current Profession.* These are the technical competencies that give you the *ability* to do your job. The skills needed to complete a task and the know-how to use them productively and efficiently.

   These *technical skills* are mandatory if you want to land a job within your profession. *Technical skills*, while transferable, vary from profession to profession, so many of your current *technical skills* will only be transferable within your current profession.

2. *Transferable Skills That Apply in All Professions.* The set of skills that underlies your ability to execute the *technical skills* of your job effectively, whatever your job might be. They are the foundation of all the professional success you will experience in this and any other career (including dream and entrepreneurial careers) that you may pursue over the years.

3. *Professional Values.* Transferable skills are complemented by an equally important set of *professional values* that are highly prized by employers. *Professional values* are an interconnected set of core beliefs that enable professionals to determine the right judgment call for any given situation.

The importance of *transferable skills* and *professional values* led to an entirely new approach to interviewing and the science of employee selection: behavioral interviewing. These behavioral interviewing techniques (discussed in detail in *Knock 'em Dead: The Ultimate Job Search Guide* and *Knock 'em Dead: Secrets and Strategies for Success in an Uncertain World*) now predominate in the selection process because of their ability to determine whether you possess those *transferable skills* and *professional values*.

A Review of the Transferable Skills and Professional Values

As you read through the following breakdown of each *transferable skill* and *professional value* you may, for example, read about *communication*, and think, "Yes, I can see how communication skills are important in all jobs and at all levels of the promotional ladder, and, hallelujah, I have good communication skills." If so, take time to recall examples of your *communication skills* and the role they play in the success of your work.

You might then read about *multitasking skills* and realize that you need to improve in this area. Whenever you identify a *transferable skill* that needs work, you have found a *professional development project*: improving that skill. Your attention to those areas will pay off for the rest of your working life, no matter how you make a living.

Certain *transferable skills* and *professional values* are seen as integral to success in every job, at every level, in every profession, everywhere in the world. The full list includes:

Communication	Motivation
Critical thinking	Determination
Multitasking	Integrity
Teamwork	Productivity
Creativity	Systems and Procedures
Leadership	

There are certain keywords and phrases that evoke these skills that you see in almost every job posting: *communication skills*, *multitasking skills*, works closely with others, *creativity*, *critical thinking*, *motivation*, *integrity*, and so on. They are so commonly used that some people dismiss them as meaningless. Far from being meaningless, they represent a secret language that few job hunters ever show that they understand. The ones who do "get it" are also the ones who get the job offers.

These keywords and phrases represent the skills that enable you to do your job well, whatever your job may be. They are known as *transferable skills* and *professional values* because no matter what the job, the profession, or the elevation of that job, these skills make the difference between success and failure. They factor into the successful execution of every aspect of your daily activities at work.

Take a few moments and compare this list of *transferable skills* and *professional values* against the responsibilities of your job as your "customers" have defined them (see your Target Job Deconstruction exercises), and identify which of the *transferable skills* helps you execute each of the job's responsibilities effectively.

Transferable Skills

The National Association of Colleges and Employers (NACE), which is made up of major corporation recruiters and university career services professionals, in agreement with the accepted thinking on these issues, has defined seven *transferable skills* that every professional entering the workplace must have in order to succeed. These seven include: *technical*, *communication*, *teamwork*, *critical thinking*, *multitasking* (time management and organization), *leadership*, and *creativity skills*.

Technical Skills

The *technical skills* of your job are the foundation of success within your current profession; without them you won't even land a job, much less keep it for long or win a promotion. They speak to your *ability* to do the job—the essential skills necessary for the day-to-day execution of your duties. These *technical skills* vary from profession to profession and do not necessarily refer to anything technical or to technology.

However, one of the *technical skills* essential to every job is technological competence. You must be proficient in all the technology and Internet-based applications relevant to your work. Even when you are not working in a technology field, strong *technology skills* will enhance your stability and help you leverage professional growth.

Some of your *technology skills* will only be relevant within your current profession, while others (Word, Excel, PowerPoint, to name the obvious) will be transferable across all industry and professional lines. Staying current with the essential *technical* and *technology skills* of your chosen career path is the cornerstone of your professional stability and growth.

Critical Thinking Skills

As I noted in the previous chapter, your job, whatever it is, exists to solve problems and to prevent problems from arising within your area of expertise. *Critical thinking*, *analytical*, or *problem-solving skills* represent a systematic approach to dealing with the challenges presented by your work. *Critical thinking skills* allow you to think through a problem, define the challenge and its possible solutions, and then evaluate and implement the best solution from all available options.

Fifty percent of the success of any project is in the preparation; *critical thinking* is at the heart of that preparation. In addition, using *critical thinking* to properly define a problem always leads to a better solution.

Communication Skills

Every professional job today demands good *communication skills*, but what are they? When the professional world talks about *communication skills*, it is referring to four primary skills and four supportive skills.

The primary *communication skills* are:

- Verbal skills—what you say and how you say it
- Listening skills—listening to understand, rather than just waiting your turn to talk
- Writing skills—clear written communication creates a lasting impression of who you are and is essential for success in any professional career
- Technological communication skills—your ability to evaluate the protocols, strengths, and weaknesses of alternative communication media, and then to choose the medium appropriate to your audience and message

The four supportive *communication skills* are:

- Grooming and dress—these tell others who you are and how you feel about yourself.
- Social graces—how you behave toward others in all situations; this defines your professionalism.
- Body language—this displays how you're feeling deep inside; it's a form of communication that precedes your speech. For truly effective communication, what your mouth says must be in harmony with what your body says.
- Emotional IQ—your emotional self-awareness, your maturity in dealing with others in the full range of human interaction.

Communication skills also go hand in hand with *critical thinking skills* to accurately process incoming information and enable you to present your outgoing verbal messaging persuasively in light of the interests and sophistication of your audience so that it is understood and accepted. If you develop competency in all eight of the subsets that together comprise *communication skills*, you'll gain enormous control over what you can achieve, how you are perceived, and what happens in your life.

Multitasking

This is one of today's most desirable skills. According to numerous studies, however, the *multitasking* demands of modern professional life are causing massive frustration and meltdowns for professionals everywhere. The problem is NOT *multitasking*;

the problem is the assumption that *multitasking* means being reactive to *all* incoming stimuli and therefore jumping around from one task to another as the emergency of the moment dictates. Such a definition of *multitasking* would of course leave you feeling that wild horses are attached to your extremities and tearing you limb from limb.

Few people understand what *multitasking* abilities are built on: sound *time-management* and *organizational* abilities. Here are the basics:

Establish Priorities
Multitasking is based in three things:

1. Being organized
2. Establishing priorities
3. Managing your time

The Plan, Do, Review Cycle
At the end of every day, review your day:

- What happened: A.M. and P.M.?
- What went well? Do more of it.
- What went wrong? How do I fix it?
- What projects do I need to move forward tomorrow?
- Rank each project. A = must be completed tomorrow. B = good to be completed tomorrow. C = if there is spare time after A and B priorities.
- Make a prioritized To Do list.
- Stick to it.

Doing this at the end of the day keeps you informed about what you have achieved, and lets you know that you have invested your time in the most important activities today and will do so again tomorrow. That peace of mind helps you feel better, sleep better, and come in tomorrow focused and ready to rock.

Teamwork
Companies depend on teams because the professional world revolves around the complex challenges of making money, and such complexities require teams of people to provide ongoing solutions. This means that you must work efficiently and respectfully with other people who have totally different responsibilities, backgrounds, objectives, and areas of expertise. It's true that individual initiative is important, but

as a professional, much of the really important work you do will be done as a member of a group. Your long-term stability and success require that you learn the arts of cooperation, team-based decision-making, and team communication.

Teamwork demands that a commitment to the team and its success comes first. This means you take on a task because it needs to be done, not because it makes you look good.

As a team player, you:

- Always cooperate.
- Always make decisions based on team goals.
- Always keep team members informed.
- Always keep commitments.
- Always share credit, never blame.

If you become a successful leader in your professional life, it's a given that you were first a reliable team player, because a leader must understand the dynamics of *teamwork* before she can leverage them. When *teamwork* is coupled with the other *transferable skills* and *professional values*, *it results in greater responsibility and promotions.*

Leadership Skills

Leadership is the most complex of all the *transferable skills* and combines all the others. As you develop *teamwork skills*, notice how you are willing to follow true leaders, but don't fall in line with people who don't respect you and who don't have your best interests at heart. When others believe in your competence, and believe you have everyone's success as your goal, they will follow you. When your actions inspire others to think more, learn more, do more, and become more, you are becoming a leader. This will ultimately be recognized and rewarded with promotion into and up the ranks of management. Here's how other *transferable skills* factor into *leadership skills*:

- Your job as a leader is to help your team succeed, and your *teamwork skills* give you the smarts to pull a team together as a cohesive unit.
- Your *technical* expertise, *critical thinking*, and *creativity skills* help you correctly define the challenges your team faces and give you the wisdom to guide them toward solutions.
- Your *communication skills* enable your team to *buy into* your directives and goals. There's nothing more demoralizing than a leader who can't clearly articulate why you're doing what you're doing.

- Your *creativity* (discussed next) comes from the wide frame of reference you have for your work and the profession and industry in which you work, enabling you to come up with solutions that others might not have imagined.
- Your *multitasking skills*, based on sound *time-management* and *organizational* abilities, enable you to create a practical blueprint for success. They also allow your team to take ownership of the task and deliver the expected results on time.

Leadership is a combination and outgrowth of all the *transferable skills* plus the clear presence of all the *professional values* we are about to discuss. Leaders aren't born; they are self-made. And just like anything else, it takes hard work.

Creativity

Your *creativity* comes from the frame of reference you have for your work, profession, and industry. This wide frame of reference enables you to see the *patterns* that lie behind challenges and so connect the dots and come up with solutions that others might not have seen. Others might be too closely focused on the specifics of the issue—thus, they don't have that holistic frame of reference that enables them to step back and view the issue in its larger context.

There's a big difference between *creativity* and just having ideas. Ideas are like headaches: We all get them once in a while, and like headaches they can disappear as mysteriously as they arrived. *Creativity*, on the other hand, is the ability to develop those ideas with the strategic and tactical know-how that brings them to life. Someone is seen as creative when his ideas produce tangible results. Other *transferable skills* complement *creativity*. *Creativity* springs from:

- Your *critical thinking skills*, applied within an area of technical expertise (an area where your *technical skills* give you knowledge of what works and what doesn't).
- Your *multitasking skills*, which, in combination with your *critical thinking* and *technical skills*, allow you to break down your challenge into specific steps and determine which approach is best.
- Your *communication skills*, which allow you to explain your approach and its building blocks persuasively to your target audience.
- Your *teamwork* and *leadership skills*, which enable you to enlist others and bring the idea to fruition.

Creative approaches to challenges can take time or can come fully formed in a flash, but the longer you work on developing the supporting skills that bring *creativity* to life, the more often they *will* come fully formed and in a flash. Here are five rules for building *creativity skills* in your professional life:

1. **Whatever you do in life, engage in it fully.** Commit to developing competence in everything you do, because the wider your frame of reference for the world around you, the more you will see the patterns and connectivity in your professional world, delivering the higher-octane fuel you need to propel your ideas to acceptance and reality.

2. **Learn something new every day.** Treat the pursuit of knowledge as a way of life. Absorb as much as you can about everything. Learning exercises your brain, filling your mind with information and contributing to that ever-widening field of vision that allows you to overcome challenges. The result is that you will make connections others won't and develop solutions that are seen as magically creative.

3. **Catch ideas as they occur.** Note them in your smartphone or on a scrap of paper. Anything will do as long as you capture the idea.

4. **Welcome restrictions in your world.** They make you think, they test the limits of your skills and the depth of your frame of reference; they truly encourage *creativity*. Ask any successful business leader, entrepreneur, writer, artist, or musician.

5. **Don't spend your life glued to Facebook or TV.** You need to live life, not watch it go by out of the corner of your eye. If you do watch television, try to learn something or motivate yourself with science, history, or biography programming. If you go online, do it with purpose.

Building *creativity skills* enables you to bring your ideas to life; and the development of each of these seven interconnected *transferable skills* will help you bring your dreams to life.

Professional Values

Professional values are an interconnected set of core beliefs that enable professionals to determine the right judgment call for any given situation. Highly prized by employers, this value system also complements and is integral to the *transferable skills*.

Motivation and Energy

Motivation and *energy* express themselves in your engagement with and enthusiasm for your work and profession. They involve an eagerness to learn and grow professionally and a willingness to take the rough with the smooth in pursuit of meaningful goals. *Motivation* is invariably expressed by the *energy* you demonstrate in your work. If you're motivated, you always give that extra effort to get the job done right.

Commitment and Reliability

These words represent your dedication to your profession and the empowerment that comes from knowing how your part contributes to the whole. Your *commitment* expresses itself in your *reliability*. The *committed* professional is willing to do whatever it takes to get a job done, whenever and for however long it takes to get the job done. Doing so might include tackling duties that don't appear in his job description and that might be perceived by less enlightened colleagues as "beneath them."

Determination

The *determination* you display with the travails of your work speaks of a resilient professional who does not back off when a problem or situation gets tough. It's a *professional value* that marks you as someone who chooses to be part of the solution.

The *determined* professional has decided to make a difference with his or her presence every day, because it is the *right* thing to do.

She is willing to do whatever it takes to get a job done, and she will demonstrate that *determination* on behalf of colleagues who share the same values.

Pride and Integrity

If a job's worth doing, it's worth doing right. That's what *pride* in your work really means: attention to detail and a *commitment* to doing your very best. *Integrity* applies to all your dealings, whether with coworkers, management, customers, or vendors. Honesty really *is* the best policy.

Productivity

A true professional always works toward *productivity* in her areas of responsibility, through efficiencies of time, resources, money, and effort.

Economy

Remember the word "frugal"? It doesn't have to be associated with poverty or shortages. It means making the most of what you've got, using everything with the greatest efficiency. Companies that know how to be frugal with their resources will prosper in good times and in bad, and if you know how to be frugal, you'll do the same.

Systems and Procedures

This is a natural outgrowth of all the other *transferable skills* and *professional values*. Your *commitment* to your profession in all these ways gives you an appreciation of the need for *systems* and *procedures* and their implementation only after careful thought. You understand and always follow the chain of command. You don't implement your own "improved" procedures—or encourage others to do so—without first talking them over with the group and getting proper approvals. If ways of doing things don't make sense or are interfering with efficiency and profitability, you work through the system to get them changed.

Developing Skills Is Worth the Effort

Development of *transferable skills* and *professional values* supports your enlightened self-interest, because your efforts will be repaid with better job security and improved professional horizons. The more you are engaged in your career, the more likely you are to join the inner circles that exist in every department and company, and that's where the plum assignments, raises, and promotions live.

Anyone seen to embody these *transferable skills* and *professional values* will be known and respected as a consummate professional.

That you have these admirable traits is one thing; that *I* know you have them, well, that's another matter. You need to:

- Develop these skills and values.
- Make them a living dimension of your professional persona.
- Understand how each enables you to do every aspect of your job just that little bit better.
- Reference them subtly in your resume and other written communications.
- Reference them appropriately in your meetings with employers as the underlying skills that enable you to do your work well.

Examples of your application of these skills or the impact of these values on your work can be used in your resume, cover letters, and as illustrative answers to questions in interviews. But most importantly, these skills must become a part of you, for they will bring you success in everything you do.

Identifying Your Competitive Difference

To win job offers, you need to differentiate yourself from other candidates. The following questionnaire will help you identify all the factors that help make you unique. Each of these is a component of your *professional brand*.

You aren't going to discover anything earth-shattering here, just a continuum of behaviors and beliefs you've always had—but the value of which you've perhaps never understood. It'll be a series of those, "Of course, I knew that" moments.

COMPLETE THE COMPETITIVE DIFFERENCE QUESTIONNAIRE ONSCREEN

An expandable version of this questionnaire is available in Microsoft Word at www.knockemdead.com on the resume advice page under the title: The Competitive Difference Questionnaire.

THE COMPETITIVE DIFFERENCE QUESTIONNAIRE

List and prioritize the transferable skills, behaviors, and values that best capture the essence of the professional you.

_____

_____

_____

_____

Which of the transferable skills, behaviors, and values have you identified for further professional development? What are you going to do about it?

_____

_____

_____

_____

What skills/behaviors/values or other characteristics do you share with top performers in your department/profession?

_____

_____

_____

_____

What have you achieved with these qualities?

_____

_____

_____

_____

What makes you different from others with whom you have worked?

_____

_____

_____

_____

What do you see as your four most defining transferable skills and professional values and how does each help your performance?

_____

_____

_____

_____

How do your most defining professional traits help you contribute to the team?

1. _____

2. _____

3. _____

4. _____

How do your most defining professional traits help you contribute to your departmental goals and/or help you support your boss?

1. _____

2. _____

3. _____

4. _____

Why do you stand out in your job/profession?

_____

_____

_____

_____

If you realize you don't stand out and you want to, explain in a few sentences why the people you admire stand out. What plans do you have for change?

_____

_____

_____

_____

In what ways are you better than others at your workplace who hold the same title?

_____

_____

_____

_____

What excites you most about your professional responsibilities?

_____

_____

_____

_____

What are your biggest achievements in these areas?

_____

_____

_____

_____

What do your peers say about you?

_____

_____

_____

_____

What does management say about you?

_____

_____

_____

_____

What do your reports say about you?

_____

_____

_____

_____

What are your top four professional skills?

Skill #1: _____

Quantifiable achievements with this skill:_____

Skill #2: _____

Quantifiable achievements with this skill:_____

Skill #3: _____

Quantifiable achievements with this skill:_____

Skill #4: _____

Quantifiable achievements with this skill:_____

What are your top four leadership skills?

Skill #1: _____

Quantifiable achievements with this skill:_____

Skill #2: _____

Quantifiable achievements with this skill:_____

Skill #3: _____

Quantifiable achievements with this skill:_____

Skill #4: _____

Quantifiable achievements with this skill:_____

What do you believe are the three key deliverables of your job?

1. _____

2. _____

3. _____

What gives you greatest satisfaction in the work you do?

_____

_____

_____

_____

What **value** does your combination of transferable skills, professional values, and achievements enable you to bring to your targeted employers?

_____

_____

_____

_____

Now compile endorsements. Looking at each of your major areas of responsibility throughout your work history, write down any positive verbal or written commentary others have made on your performance.

_____

_____

_____

_____

After rereading your answers, make three one-sentence statements that capture the essence of the professional you and your competitive difference.

_____

_____

_____

Take these three statements and rework them into one sentence. This is your competitive difference.

_____

Once you have completed the Competitive Difference Questionnaire and identified what your competitive difference is, you'll feel a new awareness of the *professional you*. The next step is to weave this new awareness and your competitive difference into all your job search communications and, in the process, give form to your brand.

A True and Truthful Brand

You have to be able to deliver on the brand you create. It must be based on your possession of the *technical skills* of your profession, those *transferable skills* that you take with you from job to job, and the *professional values* that permeate your approach to professional life.

It is all too easy to overpromise, and while an employer might initially be attracted by the pizzazz of your resume, whether or not you live up to its value proposition decides the length and quality of the relationship.

If a box of cereal doesn't live up to the brand's hype, you simply don't buy it again; but if you sell yourself into the wrong job with exaggerations or outright lies, it is likely to cost you that job—plus you risk the possibility of collateral career damage that can follow you for years.

Benefits of a Defined Professional Brand

Understanding the skills and attributes demanded for professional success might be the most immediately recognizable benefit of a defined *professional brand*, but your *professional brand* is also extremely valuable for your long-term survival and success. Knowing who you are, what you offer, and how you want to be perceived will differentiate you from others. And because you understand yourself and can communicate this understanding, you will have a professional presence.

Your Professional Brand and the Long Haul

Globalization has made your job less secure than ever, yet you are a financial entity that must survive over what will be at least a half century of work life. So while you develop an initial *professional brand* as part of your job search strategy, you don't want to shelve it once you've landed a new job.

In this new, insecure world of work, it makes sense to maintain visibility within your profession. It is nothing more than intelligent market positioning for the *professional brand* that you begin to define in this job search through your resume, cover letters, and other job search communications. This gradually evolving *professional brand* should become an integral part of the professional profile you show to the world on LinkedIn and other professional networking sites. Your brand raises your credibility and visibility within your profession as well as within the recruitment industry, making you more desirable as an employee and increasing your options.

The professionals who survive and prosper over the long haul are always people who do that little extra to make sure that they achieve their goals. When you complete the work in this chapter, you will have achieved a greater sense of self-awareness than you have ever had before. You will know exactly what you have to offer the professional world, and when you know where you stand and where you want to get in life, you can form the road map that will guide you on your journey to your destination.

GET A FREE RESUME REVIEW FROM MARTIN YATE!
Go to the website of the store where you bought the book, write an honest review,
and send the link with your resume to *MartinYate@KnockEmDead.com*.

Chapter 5

ELEMENTS OF A GREAT COVER LETTER

There is a fine line between pride in achievement and insufferable arrogance when writing about your experiences and who you are as a professional.

Now that you have a clearer idea of what makes you different, and you have captured that in a personal branding statement, you're ready to reflect this in your cover letters and all the other types of letters you use to differentiate your candidacy during the job hunt. Incidentally, you're also ready to reflect that understanding in your resume; but for that story, see the latest edition of *Knock 'em Dead Resumes*.

Differences Between Electronic and Print Cover Letters

Today's workplace can demand fifty or more hours weekly from busy, multitasking professionals. Everyone is busy; everyone is distracted. Corporate executives often base decisions on whether to return a call or respond to an email on the first few words of the message. They figure that if you can't cut to the chase, they shouldn't have to waste their time: Your communication inadequacies aren't their problem. Your cover letter and resume, whether sent by email or snail mail, competes for the attention of this audience. The key to successful communications is to construct clear, well-ordered, compelling, cut-to-the-chase letters.

A cover letter is a narrative of sequenced sentences organized around a single goal: to build a bridge of connectivity between you and the recipient and get your resume read with serious attention.

While you will likely need to create more than one type of cover letter, start by creating one general letter first. You can then use this letter as a template to cut, paste, and otherwise adapt to create other letters for different purposes. It should be brief and focus on the employer's needs, the "must-haves."

Cover Letter Ingredients

Your letters will be most effective when you do each of the following:

1. Address someone by name—whenever possible, find someone involved in the recruitment and selection cycle, ideally a hiring manager: as noted, typically 1–3 management levels above your title.
2. Mention something you have discovered in common between you and the recipient, the job, or the company.
3. Explain why you are writing, tailoring the letter to the reader/job/company as much as is practicable.
4. Include information relevant to the job you are seeking. If you completed the TJD exercise earlier in this book, you will recognize that this is possible even when you do not have a job posting.
5. Show concern, interest, and pride in your work; the branding exercises from the previous chapter will help you with this.
6. Maintain a balance between professionalism and friendliness.
7. Ask for the next step in the process clearly and without apology or arrogance.

Before discussing formatting, let's take a minute to talk in more detail about some of these issues.

What Makes a Cover Letter Work?

Your first step is to grab the reader's attention. Whenever possible, your letter should start with a personalized greeting. Email has increased the ease of written communication and relaxed a number of letter-writing rules, but you must always use a greeting/salutation to open your letter and set a professional tone. If you do not start your letter with a greeting, you are immediately seen as someone who does not have a grasp of business communication or basic social graces. Because written communication is so important in today's workplace, a lack of salutation can get your letter ignored. That's why you want to open the letter by using a person's name, spelled correctly and using one of the following forms:

- Dear Mr. Yate, (standard)
- Hello, Mr. Yate, (more casual, but still okay; not as acceptable in the professions of law, medicine, and education)
- Dear Martin Yate, or Hello, Martin Yate, (acceptable if you are an experienced professional, but not so much if you are at the entry level or in your first two or three years in the professional workplace)

Do not use first names (Hello, Martin or Dear Carole) when you haven't communicated with the reader before. First names are okay once you have spoken and you have been encouraged to use first names, when you are of similar age and professional standing. If you are younger, and even if you might have been encouraged to use first names, only do so in person; in writing, use a more formal address. It is a sign of respect that is invariably appreciated.

Starting the Letter

Everything you need to say must be short and to the point so that your copy never exceeds one page. At the same time, you want to find common ground with your reader and present yourself in the best way. Use the first paragraph to introduce yourself with conviction and establish your reason for writing, perhaps integrating a phrase that foreshadows the opening brand statement from your resume.

Here are a few examples:

"Our mutual friend Carole Mraz over at C-Soft told me to say hello. You and I haven't spoken before, but Carole thinks we might have an interesting conversation, especially if you anticipate the need for an industrious young marketing acolyte who comes equipped with a great education, two ears and one mouth, and a great desire to start at the bottom learning from an acknowledged master in the field."

"Our mutual colleague, John Stanovich, felt my skills and abilities would be valuable to your company . . ."

"The manager of your San Francisco office, Pamela Bronson, suggested I contact you regarding the opening for a _____ ."

"I received your name from Henry Charles, the branch manager of Savannah Bank, last week, and he suggested I contact you. In case the resume he forwarded is caught up in the mail, I enclosed another."

"Arthur Gold, your office manager and my neighbor, thought I should contact you about the upcoming opening in your accounting department."

"A colleague of mine, Diane Johnson, recommended your recruiting firm to me, as you recently assisted her in a strategic career move. I understand that your firm specializes in the consumer products industry."

"I met you briefly at the import/export symposium last _____ and really resonated with your comments about productivity being pulled down by sloppy communications. As I am looking to harness my _____ years of logistics expertise to an organization with a major role in global distribution . . ."

When You Have No Referral and No Job Posting

"I have been researching the leading local companies in _____, and the name of _____ Products keeps coming up as a top company. This confirmed an opinion I've developed over my three years as a committed distance-learning educator."

"Right after my mentor mentioned _____ as one of the top companies in our industry, I saw you speak at the association meeting last year. I really resonated with your comments about productivity, and as I am looking to harness my _____ years of logistics expertise to a major player, I felt this was the right time to introduce myself."

"I understand you are a manager who likes to get things done, and who needs competent, focused, goal-oriented employees . . ."

"I'm focused on finding the right boss to bring out the best in a consistently top-producing _____. I am a highly motivated producer who wants to make a contribution as part of the hard-driving team of the industry leader.

"I thought the best way to demonstrate my drive and creativity was to get you my resume in this priority mail envelope. I also sent it to you by email and uploaded it to your company resume bank, but sales is all about stacking the odds . . . and I also knew you'd appreciate a break from the computer screen."

"I've been meaning to contact you ever since I attended/read/heard about _____. It encouraged me to do a little research, which has convinced me that you are the kind of company I want to be associated with, and that I have the kind of analytical focus coupled with creative drive that can be success-fully applied to your current projects."

"I have been following the performance of your company in Mutual Funds Newsletter. *With my experience working for one of your direct competitors in the critical area of customer service, I know I could make significant contributions . . . I am detail oriented, a problem solver, and used to working with varied, often frustrated customers."*

"Recently, I have been researching the local _____ industry. My search has been focused on looking for companies that are respected in the field and that prize an employee's commitment to professional development. I am such an individual and you are clearly such a company. I bring sound technical skills, strong business acumen, and sound management skills for complex technical projects in a fast-paced environment."

"Although I am currently employed by one of your major competitors, I must admit that I was captivated by your company's mission statement when I visited your website."

"Within the next few weeks, I will be moving from New York to _____. Having researched the companies in _____, I know that you are the company I want to talk to because . . ."

"The state of the industry in _____ changes so rapidly that it is tough for most professionals to keep up. The attached resume will demonstrate that I am an exception and eager to bring my experience as a _____ to work for your company."

When You Are Responding to a Job Posting

"Your job posting #23567 cited the need for drive and creativity. I thought a good way to demonstrate my drive and creativity was to get you my resume in this priority mail envelope. Of course, I sent it to you by email as well, but marketing

communications is all about psychology and results . . . so I knew you'd get the message, appreciate the contrarian thinking, and enjoy a break from the computer screen."

"I read your job posting on your company's website on January 5th and felt I had to respond . . ."

"Your online job posting regarding a _____ on _____ .com caught my eye, and your company name caught my attention."

"This email, and my attached resume, is in response to your job posting on _____."

"I read your advertisement in the Daily Gotham *on October 6th for a _____ and, after researching your company website, felt I had to write . . ."*

"Reference job #C/AA 5670. As you compare your requirements for a _____ with my attached resume, you will see that my entire background matches your requirements exactly."

"This letter and attached resume are in response to your posting in _____."

"I was excited to see your opening for the accounting vacancy (job #S9854) on _____.com. As my attached resume demonstrates, the open position is a perfect match for my fifteen years' payroll, general ledger, and accounts receivable experience."

"While browsing the jobs database on _____.com, I was intrigued by your Regional Sales Manager job posting."

Presenting Yourself

If you haven't managed to build the reason for writing into your opening, as you just read in some of the above examples, introduce it now and go on to identify something desirable about the *professional you.*

"I am writing because . . ."

"My reason for contacting you . . ."

". . . you may be interested to know . . ."

"If you are seeking a _____, you will be interested to know . . ."

"I would like to talk to you about your staffing needs for _____ and how I might be able to contribute to your department's goals."

"If you have an opening for someone in this area, you will see that my resume demonstrates a person of unusual dedication, efficiency, and drive."

You then go on to define the kind of work you do with a brief statement and/or two to three statements that highlight your capabilities. With a short paragraph or a couple of bullets, you might highlight one or two special contributions or achievements. These can include any qualifications, contributions, and attributes that brand you as someone with talent and energy to offer.

You can also use this part of the letter to address an aspect of a particular job opening that is not addressed in your resume, and for some reason cannot be addressed there at the moment.

Or you can use the cover letter to emphasize a priority requirement(s) from the posting.

"In my resume you will find proof points for my PR acumen, including:
- *"Demonstrated track record of strategic communications and influential public relations*
- *"Accomplished media relations and story placement, from ABC World News Tonight to ZDNet*
- *"Team, account, budget, client, and C-level executive management*
- *"Client loyalty and satisfaction*
- *"Knowledge of high-tech industry and players*
- *"New business success*
- *"Self-motivated team player"*

"Although I am currently employed by one of your competitors, I have kept my eye open for an opportunity to join your organization. Over the past year I have:

- "Built a sales force of seven reps, reduced turnover, and increased individual productivity an average of 14 percent
- "Implemented a customer service plan that successfully reduced client turnover by 18 percent
- "Initiated warranty tracking, increasing upsell by 7 percent
- "Increased revenue by $4.3 million"

"As a Marketing Director with twelve years of experience in consumer products, I have:
- "Doubled revenues in just eighteen months
- "Introduced a new product that captured a 38 percent market share
- "Successfully managed a $5 million ad budget"

"I have an economics background from Columbia and employ cutting-edge quantitative analysis strategies to approach cyclical fluctuations. This has enabled me to consistently call all major peaks and valleys in the last twelve years."

"I noticed from your posting that training experience in a distance-learning environment would be a plus. You will see in my enclosed resume that I have five years' experience writing and producing sales and management training materials in new media."

"You are looking for a database administrator with experience in intranet implementation and management. As my attached resume demonstrates, I have done this type of work for six years with a regional organization on a platform of 15,000 users:
- "Desk technology upgrades
- "Responsible for hardware and peripheral selection
- "Coordinated installation of workstations
- "Trained users
- "Full upgrade achieved under budget and within deadline. Savings to company: $25,000"

You want the reader to move from your letter to the resume already primed with the feeling that you can do this job; the reference to a job's key requirement does just that. Since you want the reader to move quickly to your resume, brevity is important. Leave your reader wanting more; the letter doesn't sell you—that's the resume's job—but it should position you for serious consideration. Whet the reader's appetite, no more.

Make It Clear to the Reader That You Want to Talk

Explain when, where, and how you can be contacted. You can also be proactive by telling the reader that you intend to follow up at a certain point in time if contact has not been established by then. Just as you worked to create a strong opening, make sure your closing carries the same conviction. It is the reader's last personal impression of you, so make it strong, make it tight, and make it obvious that you are serious about entering into meaningful conversation.

Useful phrases include:

"It would be a pleasure to give you more information about my qualifications and experience . . ."

"I welcome the opportunity to discuss your specific projects and explore the possibility of joining your team."

"I look forward to discussing our mutual interests further . . ."

"I prefer not to use my employer's time taking personal calls at work, so instead you can reach me at _____."

"I will be in your area around the 20th, and will call you prior to that date. I would like to arrange . . ."

"I have pasted and attached my resume for your review and will call you in the next couple of days to discuss any openings for which your firm is currently conducting searches."

"I hope to speak with you further, and will call the week of _____ to follow up."

"The chance to meet with you would be a privilege and a pleasure, so to this end I shall call you on _____."

"I look forward to speaking with you further, and will call in the next few days to see when our schedules will permit a face-to-face meeting."

"May I suggest a personal meeting where you can have the opportunity to examine the person behind the resume?"

"My credentials and achievements are a matter of record that I hope you will examine in depth when we meet. You can reach me at _____."

"I look forward to examining any of the ways you feel my background and skills would benefit [name of organization]. I look forward to hearing from you."

"Resumes help you sort out the probables from the possibles, but they are no way to judge the caliber of an individual. I would like to meet you and demonstrate that I have the professional personality that makes for a successful _____."

"I expect to be in your area on Tuesday and Wednesday of next week, and wonder which day would be best for you. I will call to determine. In the meantime, I would appreciate your treating my application as confidential, since I am currently employed."

"With my training and hands-on experience, I know I can contribute to _____, and want to talk to you about it in person. When may we meet?"

"After reading my resume, you will know something about my background. Yet you will still need to determine whether I am the one to help you with current problems and challenges. I would like an interview to discuss my ability to make meaningful contributions to your department's goals."

"You can reach me at [home/alternate #] to arrange an interview. I know that your time investment in meeting with me will be repaid amply."

"Thank you for your time and consideration; I hope to hear from you shortly."

"May I call you for an interview in the next few days?"

"A brief phone call will establish whether or not we have mutual interest. Recognizing the demands of your schedule, I will make that call before lunch on Tuesday."

Some people feel it is powerful in the closing to state a date—"I'll call you on Friday if we don't speak before"—or a date and time—"I'll call you on Friday at 10 A.M. if we don't speak before" when they will follow up with a phone call. The logic is that you demonstrate that your intent is serious, that you are organized, and that you plan your time effectively, all of which are desirable behavioral traits and support the brand of a goal-oriented and consummate professional.

A complete idiot of a resume writer once said that an employer would be offended by being "forced" to sit and await this call. In more than thirty years of involvement in the hiring process, as a headhunter, as a hiring manager, as an HR executive, and as a writer on these issues who speaks to executives all over the world, I have never met anyone who felt constrained to wait by the phone for such a call. What sometimes *does* get noticed, though, is the person who doesn't follow through on a commitment to call as promised. Therefore, if you use this approach, keep your promise: It's part of the value proposition in your *professional brand*.

Now that you have a frame of reference for the factors that impact cover letters and any other job search letters, let's move on to the nuts and bolts of making them work. Later in the book you'll find examples of different types of cover letters: follow-up letters; networking letters; thank-you letters; resurrection letters; and acceptance, rejection, and resignation letters. You'll also find ready-to-use Microsoft Word job search letter templates in the eBook version of this book at www.knockemdead.com.

A Question of Money

Recruitment advertisements sometimes request salary information—either current salary, salary requirements, or salary history. Over the years, this issue has taken far more of people's attention than it deserves.

Recruiters and hiring managers ask about your salary for two principal reasons:

1. *Because all jobs have an approved salary range* and no matter what your skills, it is hard to win an exception to an approved salary range.
2. *Because it tells about your salary trajectory*, the offer you are likely to accept, and the raises you are used to.

There are other considerations as well:

- Interviews take precious time, and managers are reluctant to waste it on candidates who could never be hired because of their salary needs.
- In a down economy, when money is tighter and companies have more candidates to choose from, it is known as a "buyer's market" and employers have far less incentive to negotiate beyond the approved salary.
- If there is an exception, it is when you are in a hot job within an in-demand professional area or you have a unique skill set that gives you a competitive edge.

Writing that your salary is "negotiable," annoys HR people. They already know salary is negotiable, and the reply doesn't answer the question they need answered.

With an in-demand job in a good economy, "negotiable" is rarely grounds for refusing to talk to a candidate, but in a buyer's market, "negotiable" might not always have the desired result.

Given this understanding, if you have the skills and you are in the approved range you'll get an interview. If you aren't . . . well, then your energies are probably better invested in finding other opportunities, but make the pitch anyway; you have nothing to lose.

When your salary requirements are requested, don't restrict yourself to one figure; instead, give yourself a range. All job openings have an approved salary *range*, so providing your own range dramatically improves your chances of fitting into the salary range that is authorized for every position.

HOW DO I DETERMINE MY SALARY RANGE?

For more on how to determine the salary range you should be sharing with employers, see the negotiation chapter in this year's edition of *Knock 'em Dead: The Ultimate Job Search Guide*.

If you are asked about your current salary and choose to answer, be honest. This isn't something you can ever fudge on. It can and does get verified. Any discrepancies can result in your being dismissed with cause, and such an event will dog your career for years. Here is one way to address the topic of money in your cover letter. You will find other examples later in the book.

> *"Depending on the job and the professional development environment, my salary requirements are in the $_____ to $_____ range, with appropriate benefits."*

Address this issue in the cover letter or in a document attached to the cover letter but never in the resume itself. This is because your resume may be kept in a database for years and your salary range may typecast you as, say, an entry-level professional in the eyes of that company's computer. Here is an example of a salary history attachment.

Salary History Attachment

Pᴀᴍᴅ Qᴍᴀᴊ ꜰ

86 Concord Street, Apt # 232 • Charlotte, NC 46776

Home (555) 555-1234 • Mobile (555) 555-1234 • me@email.com

Sᴀꜰ ᴀᴄ Oʜᴀᴊ ᴀʟᴀᴄꜰᴋ/Pᴅᴀꜰ ʟ Mᴀꜰ ᴀAᴂᴀꜰ ʟ Pᴊ ᴄʙᴀᴋᴋᴀᴄꜰ ᴀᴅ

Continuous Improvement/Lean Six Sigma/Start-Up & Turnaround Operations/

Mergers & Change Management/Process & Productivity Optimization/HR/

Logistics & Supply Chain

Sᴀᴅᴀᴊ ǫ Hᴀᴋʟ ᴄᴊ ǫ

Uꜰ ᴀʟᴀB Sʟᴀʟᴀᴋ Mᴀᴊ ᴀꜰ ᴀ Cᴄ ʜᴋ Aᴀᴊ Sʟᴀʟᴀᴄ, Cherry Point, NC—2008 to 2010

Chief Operations Officer/*** Training School Officer in Charge**

Salary—$95,309

Uꜰ ᴀʟᴀB Sʟᴀʟᴀᴋ Mᴀᴊ ᴀꜰ ᴀ Cᴄ ʜᴋ Aᴀᴊ Sʟᴀʟᴀᴄ, Futenma, Okinawa, Japan—2005 to 2008

********** Maintenance Chief—General Operations Manager/Plant Manager**

Starting Salary—$64,484/Ending Salary—$97,500

Uꜰ ᴀʟᴀB Sʟᴀʟᴀᴋ Mᴀᴊ ᴀꜰ ᴀ Cᴄ ʜᴋ Aᴀᴊ Sʟᴀʟᴀᴄ, Beaufort, SC—2001 to 2005

Plant Manager/Senior Operations Manager

Starting Salary—$49,507/Ending Salary—$64,484

Uꜰ ᴀʟᴀB Sʟᴀʟᴀᴋ Mᴀᴊ ᴀꜰ ᴀ Cᴄ ʜᴋ RᴀAᴊ ᴍᴀʟᴀꜰ A Sʟᴀʟᴀᴄ, Jacksonville, FL—1998 to 2001

Recruiting Manager

Starting Salary—$42,545/Ending Salary—$49,507

Contact Information

With an email, your return address is built into your communications and you can add a telephone number beneath your signature. A printed letter should include address, telephone number, and email address. Once you have determined a primary contact number for your job search, you must ensure that it will be answered *at all times*. There is no point in mounting a job search campaign if prospective employers can never reach you. Using your cell phone means that calls will usually get answered, but can you guarantee the voicemail and your live greeting will always be professional? If not, and you have a landline, your telephone company offers you multiple numbers and voicemails. Take advantage of this and dedicate one line exclusively to your career. Your voicemail message is important when you miss calls, or when taking a call simply isn't appropriate. Keep the message businesslike and, once recorded, replay it and listen carefully to the message for clarity, tone of voice, and recording quality. Does it present you as a clear-spoken, confident professional? Does it reflect the professional image you'd like to show to the world? Never use your company telephone or email for any job search activities, ever.

If you're sending out cover letters by email with resume attachments, be sure to hyperlink the email address in your resume. That way, anyone can send an email back to you with one click of the mouse, directly from your resume. Remember, it's all about making it easy for recruiters and hiring managers to contact you. The less work you make them do, the better your chances of success.

Chapter 6

HOW TO BUILD A COVER LETTER

There are six steps to organize the building blocks of your cover letter into a coherent, effective whole.

Step One: Identify Your Target Job

Your job search—and the resume and letters that go with it—will be incalculably more productive if you begin by clearly defining a target job that you can land and in which you can be successful. Start by identifying this target job title.

Step Two: Research the Target Job

Any evaluation of your background must begin with an understanding of what potential employers will be looking for when they come to your cover letter and resume. Collect six job postings that carry this target job title. Once you have a selection, deconstruct them as described in the Target Job Deconstruction exercise in Chapter 3.

Step Three: Review Your Most Recent Work History

When you know what your customers are looking for, and therefore what they will respond to, it's time to walk through your work history with an eye to those facets of your experience that will be of particular interest to such customers. *Knock 'em Dead Resumes* and *Knock 'em Dead: The Ultimate Job Search Guide* walk you through this process in detail. We can't do that here, but knowing what your customers want to buy (through your TJD) and how to illustrate your ability to deliver on their needs, is part of the story. For now, consider the following components, culled from the more comprehensive treatment in the other two books:

A. Current or most recent employer: Identify your current or most recent employer by name and location, and follow it with a brief description (five or six words) of the company's business/products/services.
B. Duties: Make a prioritized list of the duties/responsibilities/deliverables of this position.
C. Skills: What special skills or knowledge did you need to perform each of these tasks well? Which *transferable skills* and *professional values* helped you execute each of these tasks successfully?

- What educational background and/or credentials helped prepare you for these responsibilities?
- For each area of responsibility (deliverable), consider both the daily problems that arise and the major crises. Recall how you executed your job's responsibilities to prevent these problems from arising in the first place, and the analytical processes, subsequent actions, *transferable skills*, and successful solutions you implemented to reach successful outcomes when, despite your best efforts, these problems did arise. (More on this in Step Four.) There is a four-step technique called PSRV that you will find useful here:

P. Identify the *project* and the problem it represented, both from a corporate perspective and from the point of view of your execution of duties.

S. Identify your *solution* to the challenge and the process you implemented to deliver the solution.

R. What was the *result* of your approach and actions?

V. Finally, what was the *value* to you, the department, and the company? If you can, define this in terms of meaningful contribution: time saved, money saved, or money earned. This is not always possible, but it is very powerful whenever you can employ it.

Step Four: Consider *Transferable Skills* and *Professional Values* Used

Which *transferable skills* and *professional values* helped you succeed with this particular task? Come up with examples of how you used each particular skill in the execution of each of your major duties at this job. The examples you generate can be used not only in your job search letters, but in your resume and as illustrative answers to interview questions.

Step Five: Add Your Earlier Work History

Now repeat Step Three, the problem-solving nature of your work, and Step Four, how you used the *transferable skills* and *professional values* in your work, with each of your previous jobs. Do not skimp on this process. Everything you write might not go into the final version of your first cover letter, but all your effort will be rewarded by using the information in another letter, in your resume, or in response to an interview question. This exercise identifies the building blocks of what it takes to be successful in your profession, and the information you need at your fingertips to explain what you do objectively. The ultimate payoff is more and better job offers and a more successful career.

Step Six: Compile Endorsements

Looking at each of your major areas of responsibility throughout your work history, write down any positive verbal or written commentary others have made on your performance. As you will see in some of the sample letters in Chapter 10, praise for you that comes from someone else often has a much greater impact than anything you could come up with yourself.

Now, these compliments don't always happen that often, and you might sometimes push the accolades away. That's okay, lots of people do; but from now on, make a point of capturing them for use in the future.

QUESTIONS TO ANSWER

Comments that answer questions like these make for great endorsements: How did you work productively with coworkers, reports, and management? What different levels of people do you have to interact with to achieve your job's deliverables? What have you learned about productivity and communication from these experiences, and what does this say about you? Don't have any endorsements? Then evaluate yourself in these same areas with the Competitive Difference Questionnaire from Chapter 4, and use the results in letters, your resume, or at job interviews.

Create Punchy Sentences

Ultimately, any letter is only as good as the individual sentences that carry the message. Your goal is to communicate an energizing message and entice the reader to action. Concise, punchy sentences grab attention.

Verbs always help energize a sentence and give it that short, cut-to-the-chase feel. For example, one professional—with a number of years at the same law firm in a clerical position—had written:

"I learned to manage a computerized database."

Sounds pretty ordinary, right? Well, after looking at her job as an ongoing problem-solving exercise, certain exciting facts emerged. By using verbs and an awareness of employer interests as they relate to her target job, she was able to charge up this sentence and give it more punch. Not only that, but for the first time the writer fully understood the value of her contributions, which greatly enhanced her self-confidence in interviews:

"I analyzed and determined need for comprehensive upgrade of database, archival, and retrieval systems. Responsible for selection and installation of 'cloud-based' archival systems. Company-wide archival system upgrade completed in one year."

Notice how the verbs show that she made things happen and put flesh on the bones of that initial bare statement. Such action verbs and phrases add an air of direction, efficiency, and accomplishment to every cover letter. Succinctly, they tell the reader what you did and how well you did it.

As you recall information that will contribute to your cover letter, rewrite key phrases to see if you can give them more depth with the use of action verbs. While a cover letter is typically one page, or one screen shot, don't worry about the length right now; you can shorten it later. The process you go through helps you think out exactly what you have to offer and also creates the language and ideas you will use to explain yourself during an interview.

Vary Sentence Structure

As noted in the previous section, your letters will be most effective when they are constructed with short, punchy sentences. As a rule, try keeping your sentences under about twenty-five words; a good average is around fifteen. If your sentence is longer than the twenty-five-word mark, change it. Either shorten it through restructuring, use semicolons to save space by obviating the need for the words necessary to orient a whole new sentence, or make two sentences out of one. At the same time, you will want to avoid choppiness, so vary the length of sentences when you can.

You can also start with a short phrase ending in a colon:

- Followed by bullets of information
- Each one supporting the original phrase

These techniques are designed to enliven the reading process for readers, who always have too much to read and too little time. Here's how we can edit and rewrite the last example.

Analyzed and determined need for comprehensive upgrade of database, archival, and retrieval systems:

Responsible for software selection and compatibility issues

Responsible for selection and installation of "cloud-based" archival systems

Trained users, from managing partner through administrators

Achieved full upgrade, integration, and compliance in six months

Partner stated, "You brought us out of the dark ages, and neither you nor the firm missed a beat!"

K.I.S.S. (Keep It Simple, Stupid)

Persuading your readers to take action is challenging because many people in different companies and with different agendas see your letters and make different judgments based on those agendas. This means you must keep industry jargon to a reasonable level (especially in the initial contact letters—covers, broadcast, and the like); the rule of thumb is to use only the jargon and acronyms used in the job posting. Some readers will understand the intricacies and technicalities of your profession, but many more will not.

Within your short paragraphs and short sentences, beware of name-dropping and acronyms, such as, "I worked for Dr. A. Witherspoon in Sys. Gen. SNA 2.31." Statements like these can be too restricted to have meaning outside the small circle of specialists to whom they speak. Unless you work in a highly technical field and are sending the letter and resume to someone by name and title who you know will understand the importance of your technical language, be sure to use such phrases with discretion.

While you want your letters to have the widest possible appeal, they also need to remain personal in tone, so they don't sound like they're from Publishers Clearing House. You are not writing a novel but rather trying to capture the essence of the *professional you* in just a few brief paragraphs. Short words in short sentences help make short, gripping paragraphs—good for short attention spans!

Person and Tense

Whether you use the first or the third person for different letters depends on a few important factors:

- Getting a lot said in a small space
- Packaging your skills and credentials for the target job
- Being factual
- Capturing the essence and personality of the *professional you*

There is considerable disagreement among the "experts" about whether to write in the first or the third person, and each option has both champions and detractors. The most important point is that, whichever one you use in your letters, you must be consistent throughout that letter. For example, bullet points in all types of cover letters can be shortened and given a more immediate feel, by omitting pronouns such as *I, you, he, she, they*:

> *I analyzed and determined the need for comprehensive upgrade of database*
> can be replaced with:
> *Analyzed and determined the need for comprehensive upgrade of database*

In fact, many authorities recommend dropping pronouns as a technique that both saves space and allows you to brag about yourself without seeming boastful. It gives the impression of another party writing about you. Some feel that to use the personal pronoun—"I analyzed and determined the need for comprehensive upgrade of database . . ."—is naive, unprofessional, and smacks of boasting.

Still others recommend that you write in the first person because it makes you sound more human.

In short, there are no hard-and-fast rules—they can all work, given the many unique circumstances you will face in any given job search. It is common in resumes to cut personal pronouns, but given the personal nature of a letter, there is a danger of the message sounding too choppy without pronouns. Use whatever style works best for you and for the particular cover letter you are writing. As you will be using the personal pronoun in your letters, try not to use it in every sentence; it gets a little monotonous, and it can make you sound like an egomaniac. The mental focus should be not on "I" but on "you," the person with whom you are communicating.

A nice variation is to use the first person throughout the letter, and then end with a final few words in the third person. Make sure these final words appear in the form of an attributed quote, such as an insight into your value:

"Partner stated, 'You brought us out of the dark ages, and neither you nor the firm missed a beat!'"

Don't confuse professionalism in your job search letters with stiff-necked formality. The most effective tone is one that mixes the conversational and the formal, just as we do in our offices and on our jobs. The only overriding rule is to make the letter readable so that the reader can see a human being and a professional shining through the page.

Length

As I indicated earlier, the standard length for a cover letter is usually one page, or the equivalent length for emails; typically this is as much as you can see on your screen without scrolling. Subsequent letters stemming from verbal communications—whether over the telephone or face-to-face—should strive to keep to the one-page rule, but can run to two pages if the complexity of content demands it.

Yet, in many cases, with conscientious editing over a couple of days, that two-page letter can usually be reduced to one page without losing any of the content, and at the same time it will probably pack more punch. As my editor always says, "If in doubt, cut it out."

Having said this, I should acknowledge that all rules are made to be broken. Occasionally a two-page letter might be required, generally in one of the following instances:

1. You are at a level, or your job is of such technical complexity, such that you cannot edit down to one page without using a font size that is all but unreadable.
2. You have been contacted directly by an employer about a specific position and have been asked to present data for a specific opportunity.
3. An executive recruiter who is representing you determines that the exigencies of a particular situation warrant a dossier of such length. (Often such a letter and resume will be prepared exclusively—or with considerable input—by the recruiter.)

You'll find that thinking too much about length considerations will hamper the writing process. Think instead of the story you have to tell, and then layer fact upon fact until your tale is told. Use your words and the key phrases from this book to craft the message of your choice. When that is done, you can go back and ruthlessly cut it to the bone.

Ask yourself these questions:

- Can I cut out any paragraphs?
- Can I cut out any sentences?
- How can I reduce the word count of the longer sentences?
- Where have I repeated myself?

Whenever you can, cut something out—leave nothing but facts and action verbs! If at the end you find too much has been cut, you'll have the additional pleasure of reinstating your prose.

Chapter 7

HOW TO POLISH AND EDIT YOUR LETTERS FOR MAXIMUM IMPACT

Any job search letter is only as good as the individual sentences that carry your message. The most grammatically correct sentences in the world won't necessarily get you interviews, because they can read as though every breath of life has been squeezed out of them. Your goal is to communicate an energizing message and entice the reader to action.

A cover letter typically consists of three to five carefully constructed paragraphs. That's plenty of space to get your message across—and a second page simply won't get read.

Just as you would limit a printed cover letter to one page, you should try to keep an email cover letter to one screen: That's as compact as possible. If you cannot get your entire letter into one screen view, at least make an effort to be certain that the meat of your pitch is on that first full screen.

The amount of email traffic is growing exponentially, so hit your main points quickly and with clarity or lose your reader's attention. A good subject line grabs attention, but if the first two sentences don't succinctly state your purpose and maintain that initial attention, the reader has little reason for wasting any more precious time on the rest of your message.

Your professional business correspondence should demonstrate your written *communication skills* with powerful messaging that omits extraneous information and delivers the message in a format that is a model of clarity: easily accessible to both the eye and the mind.

Readability

Whether delivered by email or in an envelope, your resume and letter will typically arrive on a reader's desktop with a dozen other priorities. You can expect your letter to get a maximum five-second scan to see if it is worth reading; this will cover the subject line/opening sentence, spelling of the recipient's name, and general readability. If it passes the scan test, you probably have thirty seconds to make your point, and that's assuming your letter cuts to the chase and speaks to the reader's needs.

Mistakes to Avoid

Letters that never get read have four things in common:

- They have too much information crammed into the space and are difficult to read—clearly the customer doesn't come first.
- The layout is unorganized, illogical, and uneven; it looks shoddy and slapdash—and no one wants an employee like that.
- The recipient's name is misspelled—that's disrespectful.
- The letter contains typos—not acceptable in an age of spellcheckers.

Get Your Head Into Communication Mode

Your resume and cover letter will always compete for the attention of a consistently distracted audience. The good news is that while your cover letter has a difficult job to do, if you apply just a few simple tactics, you can create one that dramatically increases the impact of your accompanying resume.

Advertising copywriters, with their ability to entertain and sell us stuff we absolutely don't need in a thirty-second commercial, are arguably society's most effective communicators. They all share one common approach to their work: They get inside, and stay inside, the customer's head throughout the writing process. They focus on what features their product possesses and which benefits are most likely to appeal to the customer.

With your Target Job Deconstruction in hand, you know with considerable accuracy what your customer wants to hear about. From the Competitive Difference Questionnaire, you know what unique features and benefits you have to offer. With this self-knowledge, you have everything you need to polish the draft letters you have just created.

How Long Should It Be?

Long enough to make your point and not a word longer. The standard length for a cover letter is less than one page (or fewer than 300 words); with an email, the equivalent is typically as much as you can see on your screen without scrolling. They can also be much shorter. Here is a cover letter that gets to the point in seventy-one words:

> *"Your colleague, Bill Jacobson, suggested that I send you my resume. He mentioned that your department is looking for a database administrator with experience in intranet implementation and management. As my attached resume demonstrates, I have done that type of work for six years with a regional organization on a platform of 15,000 users. I welcome the opportunity to discuss your specific projects and explore the possibility of joining your team."*

With conscientious editing (spread over a couple of days to give you an objective distance), you can get any letter down to 300 words. The result will be a tighter letter that packs more punch.

Avoid Acronyms and Professional Slang

Every profession has its acronyms and professional slang/jargon, but there will be people in the recruitment and selection cycle who don't get it all. The acronyms and jargon have their place in your resume, but try to keep them under control in your letters.

The rule of thumb is that if the professional slang is used in the job posting, you can use it in your cover letter, because the employer is pretty much guaranteed to understand it. If not, find another way of saying it.

Give Action to Your Statements with Verbs

The focus of your letter echoes the prioritization of keywords identified in your TJD and the results of your Difference Questionnaire. These keywords are invariably nouns, but simply listing them doesn't make for an interesting story. Use verbs that show you in action:

- Responsible for all Accounts Payable
- Reduced Accounts Payable by . . .
- Streamlined Accounts Payable by . . .
- Managed all Accounts Payable . . .

Verbs always help energize a sentence and give it that short, cut-to-the-chase feel. Verbs show you in action: They give the reader a point of view, a way to see you. Verbs are an important part of creating your *professional brand* because they bring an air of direction, efficiency, and accomplishment to your written communications. Succinctly, they tell the reader *what* you did and *how well* you did it, and by implication anticipate you performing to the same standards when on the reader's payroll.

To help you in the process, here are more than 175 action verbs you can use. This list is just a beginning. Just about every word-processing program has a thesaurus; you can type any one of these words into it and get more choices for each entry.

accomplished	completed	enabled	initiated	prepared
achieved	composed	encouraged	innovated	presented
acted	computed	engineered	inspected	prioritized
adapted	conceptualized	enlisted	installed	processed
addressed	conducted	established	instigated	produced
administered	consolidated	evaluated	instituted	programmed
advanced	contained	examined	instructed	projected
advised	contracted	executed	integrated	promoted
allocated	contributed	expanded	interpreted	provided
analyzed	controlled	expedited	interviewed	publicized
appraised	coordinated	explained	introduced	published
approved	corresponded	extracted	invented	purchased
arranged	counseled	fabricated	launched	recommended
assembled	created	facilitated	lectured	reconciled
assigned	critiqued	familiarized	led	recorded
assisted	cut	fashioned	maintained	recruited
attained	decreased	focused	managed	reduced
audited	delegated	forecast	marketed	referred
authored	demonstrated	formulated	mediated	regulated
automated	designed	founded	moderated	rehabilitated
balanced	developed	generated	monitored	remodeled
budgeted	devised	guided	motivated	repaired
built	diagnosed	headed up	negotiated	represented
calculated	directed	identified	operated	researched
catalogued	dispatched	illustrated	organized	restored
chaired	distinguished	implemented	originated	restructured
clarified	diversified	improved	overhauled	retrieved
classified	drafted	increased	oversaw	revitalized
coached	edited	indoctrinated	performed	saved
collected	educated	influenced	persuaded	scheduled
compiled	eliminated	informed	planned	schooled

screened	specified	supervised	trained	validated
set	stimulated	surveyed	translated	worked
shaped	streamlined	systemized	traveled	wrote
solidified	strengthened	tabulated	trimmed	
solved	summarized	taught	upgraded	

Fonts

The font you choose has a big impact on the readability of your work. Stay away from script-like fonts, and use only those accepted as suitable for professional communication. A script may at first seem to be more visually appealing, but it can be tedious to read, and the goal is accessibility for a reader who is plowing through stacks of resumes when she gets your message.

The font(s) you choose must be used in a size legible for hiring managers. Anyone who has been staring at computer screens for ten or more years is likely to suffer from eyestrain and have problems with ten-point fonts; eleven- or twelve-point fonts are recommended.

Your branding message stays strong and consistent by using the same font choices (and paper) for your letters as you use for your resume.

The font you used for contact information and headlines in your resume is the same font you will use for your letterhead on your cover letter. The font you chose for your resume's body copy is the same as you will use for the message in your letters.

Good Fonts for Headlines/Contact Information/Signature
Arial
Century Gothic
Gill Sans
Lucida Sans
Times
Verdana

Good for Body Copy of Letters
Bodoni
Garamond
Georgia
Goudy Old Style

Note: Copy written in all capital letters, in any font, is harder to read. Use sparingly, if at all.

How to Brighten the Page

Once you decide on a font, stick with it. Apart from headlines and contact information, more than one font on a page can look confusing. You can do plenty to liven up the visual impact of the page within the variations of the font you have chosen.

All the recommended fonts come in regular, bold, italic, underlined, and bold italic, so you can vary the impact of keywords with *italics*, <u>underlined phrases</u>, and **boldface** for additional emphasis. For example, when you are sending a cover letter and resume in response to an Internet job posting or recruitment advertisement, you can bold or italicize those words used by the employer in the recruitment copy, emphasizing your match to their needs.

You should stay away from exclamation points and emoticons. In the samples section you will find little variation on the font choice beyond an occasionally italicized or bolded word. In the end, it's your judgment call. Just don't overdo the typographic pyrotechnics.

CLIP ART ALERT
Another no-no is the use of "clip art" to brighten the page. Those little quill pens and scrolls may look nifty to you, but they look amateurish to the rest of the world.

Email Considerations

Do not include your email address in the cover letter, because contact information for the medium and the date and time of your communication are entered automatically. If you are attaching a resume, your email address will be seen in the contact information there.

Subject Line

Provide a revealing and concise subject line. It should allow the receiver to immediately know who you are and what you want.

The use of a powerful subject line can mean the difference between someone opening your email or hitting the delete key. Think of it like a magazine cover, which uses splashy headlines to grab the reader and draw him into the stories inside. With email, your subject line is your headline; it draws the reader into your email. Your subject line needs to be intriguing and it also needs to be professional.

Do not use a subject line that states the obvious, like "Resume" or "Jim Smith's Resume." If you are responding to a job posting, the job title and job posting number are necessary, but just a start. Combine this factual information with a little intriguing information, such as:

Financial Analyst #MB450—CPA/MBA/8 yrs' exp.

Posting 2314—MIT Grad is interested

Job #6745—Top Sales Professional Here

Or, if there is no job posting to refer to:

IT Manager—7 yrs IT Consulting

Benefits Consultant—Nonprofit Exp in NY

Referral from Tony Banks—Product Management Job

You can also try longer subject lines, for example:

Your next Reg HR Manager—EEOC, FLSA, & ADA exp.

A message in your inbox will typically reveal a maximum of 60 characters (the above example is just 47 characters), and an opened message will show up to 150 characters. To be safe, try to get the most important part of your headline in the first 35 characters:

Your next Reg HR Manager—EEOC, FLSA

but feel free to use all this extra headline space; this example is just 144 characters:

Your next Reg HR Manager—EEOC, FLSA, ADA, OSHA. 10 years' exp. includes arbitration, campus, executive recruitment, selection, compensation, T&D

Greeting

It is unprofessional to start an email (or any business communication) without a salutation. There are basic professional courtesies that you must recognize. Don't address the recipient on a first-name basis unless you are already familiar with your contact.

Begin your messages:

Dear Tiffany Carstairs,

Or refer to a specific job, followed by salutation:

Ref Job #2376

Dear Ms. Carstairs,

Or with one of the other appropriate greetings we mentioned in Chapter 5.

Sign Off

End your emails with your name followed by contact information:

Thomas Torquemada

516.555.9374

Although there is a reply button built into every email program, some people add a hyperlinked (live) email address here on the basis that it encourages a response. If you decide to do so, place it before the telephone number:

Thomas Torquemada
ThomasTorquemada@hotmedia.com
516.555.9374

You could also finish with a signature in a script-like font:

Thomas Torquemada
ThomasTorquemada@hotmedia.com
516.555.9374

When you receive an email that contains what appears to be a real signature, it makes an impression. However, *you should never use your real signature*; with the littlest bit of technical expertise anyone could copy it, and electronic signatures can have the same legal validity as a written signature. Don't risk your online security for the sake of style. Instead, use one of the more legible script fonts. It's a nice touch that most people don't use, and it becomes part of the branding process that differentiates you. But only do this when everything else about your resume and letter package is complete and consummately professional.

Custom Stationery

A number of email programs now support the creation of customized stationery for your emails. This is a "nice to have" look when you are sending directly to an individual and all other aspects of your resume and letter are perfect. There is little point in having fancy email stationery if the wording of your letter is sloppy. It sends entirely the wrong message about who you are as a professional and works against your brand.

If you pursue the option of creating emails that look more like traditional business letters, you will follow the same rules for font choice, layout, and page color as you would sending traditional mail communications.

Paste and Attach

It is normal when sending resumes without a prior conversation to attach a Microsoft Word or PDF version of your resume and to paste an ASCII version of your resume into the email after your signature. You do this because some employers will not open attachments from people they do not know, for fear of viruses. With PDF documents, the layout is fixed and will appear exactly as you send it. With Microsoft Word, the formatting sometimes gets altered in transmission. Both ways are acceptable, and some people even attach their resume in both formats to give the reader a choice. Because of the layout issues with Microsoft Word docs, I am leaning toward using PDF.

Your cover letter will address this by saying, perhaps toward the end of your message:

"I have attached my resume in Microsoft Word [or PDF] and also pasted it below the signature in ASCII for your convenience."

MAIL MERGE ALERT FOR EMAIL AND TRADITIONAL MAIL

If you are crafting a cover letter for mass distribution, beware using the mail merge feature of a word-processing program. All too often, the program will fill in the blanks: "Dear _____" with *italics* (Dear *Fred Jones*) or ***bold italics*** (Dear ***Fred Jones***). This detracts from all your efforts to be seen in a positive light; all you've achieved is to make it clear that this is a form email, probably sent to thousands of people.

Spell-Checking Options

You can and should set your emails to check spelling before each and every message is sent, but never forget that *automatic spellcheck is not completely reliable*.

Before you send any online or print resume, cover letter, or any other job search communication, remember to proofread and get additional outside help in proofreading. Ask family and friends to review your deathless literary prose looking for typos and errors in formatting and wording to make sure that what you believe you are sending is received in the way you intended. If you want a professional editor to review your work, we offer an editing service on the resume services page at www .knockemdead.com.

Traditional Mail Still Works

Whenever you send your resume by more than one communication medium, it greatly improves your odds. With email as the standard communication medium, most managers get far less traditional mail than they used to, so when you send an email cover letter and also one by traditional mail, you at least double your chances of getting your resume read by someone in a position to interview and hire you. We all like to open the mail; it helps us get started at the beginning of the day and fills in those gaps before lunch and as we are winding down at the end of the workday.

Coordinate Your Stationery

Letter stationery should always match the color and weight of your envelopes and resume. Sending a white cover letter—even if it is your personal stationery—with a cream resume detracts from the statement you are trying to make. As for colors, white, cream, and gray are all acceptable. Do not use pastel shades unless your target job involves interaction with the very young, aged, or infirm, where your color choice may then speak to the personal sensitivity that is relevant with such professions.

Paper Quality

The quality of the paper you use matters because it affects the way others perceive you. It tells the recipient something about your values and the importance you attach to the message. Coordinating paper and quality deserves proper attention as an integral part of establishing your *professional brand*.

All the office supply superstores carry good-quality matching resume paper and envelopes. When you print out resumes, print some letterhead at the same time.

Consistency

Contact information on your letters should be the same as the contact information on your resume, and should use the same font. Likewise, the body copy of your letters will use the same font as the body copy on your resume: Matching paper and coordinated and complementary fonts speak of a person who proceeds with intent in her professional life. It is another subtle way in which you establish a *professional brand.*

All subsequent letters (follow-up letters after interviews, for example) should be on the same matching paper and envelopes, using the same matching fonts in the same or similar font sizes.

Your written communication is likely to be filed in a candidate dossier. Prior to the hiring decision, a hiring manager will review all the written materials from all the short-list candidates. A thoughtfully packaged written-communication aspect of your job search campaign will paint the picture of a top-notch professional, and the sum of your letters will become a powerful and expressive component of the total *professional you.*

What goes on the envelope affects the impact of the message inside. Over the years, I've spoken with countless managers and human resources professionals about the appearance of the envelopes they receive. Did it affect the likelihood of the letter being read and, if so, with what kind of anticipation? Here's what I heard:

"I never open letters with printed pressure-sensitive labels; I regard them as junk mail, and I simply don't have the time in my life for ill-targeted marketing attempts."

"I never open anything addressed to me by title but not by name."

"I will open envelopes and read letters or emails addressed to me by misspelled name, but I am looking with a jaundiced eye, keen for other examples of sloppiness."

"I always open correctly typed envelopes that say 'personal' and/or 'confidential,' but if they're not, I feel conned. I don't hire con artists."

"I always open neatly handwritten envelopes. What's more, I open them first, unless there's another letter that is obviously a check."

This last comment is especially interesting in an age when just about all correspondence is printed. In an entirely unscientific test, over a two-week period, every letter I had to send I sent with a hand-addressed envelope. About 50 percent of the recipients actually commented that they had not seen a handwritten envelope in ages.

If your letter is going by traditional mail and is more than one page, it should be paginated with contact information on every page, the pages stapled together with one staple in the top left-hand corner. Remember, never use company email or telephone number as contact information unless your current employer understands that you are leaving and you have permission to use company time and equipment for your search.

NEAT TRADITIONAL MAIL TACTIC

I once received an intriguing resume and cover letter. Both letter and resume had a circular red sticker attached to the top right-hand corner. It worked as a major exclamation point; I was impressed. I was even more impressed when I realized that once this left my hands, no other reader would know exactly who attached the sticker, but they *would* pay special attention to the content because of it.

Appearance Checklist

Remember that the first glance and feel of your letter can make a powerful impression. The letter's appearance should go hand in hand with its professional-sounding, clear content. Before you seal the envelope, go through this checklist:

Appearance and Formatting

❑ Does the paper measure 8½" × 11", and is it of good quality with a nice weight?
❑ Have you used white, off-white, cream, or pale gray paper?
❑ Did you use only one side of the page?
❑ Is contact information on every page?
❑ If there is more than one page, have you paginated your letter?
❑ If there is more than one page, are the pages stapled together? One staple in the top left-hand corner is the accepted protocol. Resume should *not* be stapled to cover letter.
❑ Did you spell check, grammar check, and then proofread carefully just to make sure everything's correct?

Content

❑ Does your letter state why you are writing?
❑ Is the letter tied to the target company?
❑ Does it refer to a specific job or job posting code when this is relevant?

❑ Is it focused on a target job's duties whenever possible?

❑ Does it include a reference to relevant *transferable skills* and *professional values*?

❑ Does it use verbs to show you in action, making a difference with your presence?

❑ Are your most relevant and qualifying experiences prioritized to lend strength to your letter?

❑ Have you avoided wasting more space than needed with employer names and addresses?

❑ Have you omitted any reference to reasons for leaving a particular job? Reasons for making a change might be important at the interview, but they are not relevant at this point. Use this precious space to sell, not to justify.

❑ Unless they have been specifically requested, have you removed all references to past, current, or desired salaries?

❑ Have you removed any references to your date of availability?

❑ Do you mention your highest educational attainment only if it is especially relevant, and do you mention your major only if it adds credence to the message?

❑ Have you avoided listing irrelevant responsibilities or experience?

❑ Have you given examples of your contributions/achievements, when possible?

❑ Have you avoided poor focus by eliminating all extraneous information?

❑ Is the letter long enough to whet the reader's appetite for more details, yet short enough not to satisfy that hunger?

❑ Have you let the obvious slip in, like heading your letter "Letter of Application" in big bold letters? If so, cut it.

❑ Do you have complete contact information—name, address, zip code, telephone number, and email address? Omit your current business number unless it is absolutely necessary and safe to include it. This will only be the case if your employer understands that you are leaving and you have permission to use company time and equipment for your search.

Proofing and Printing

It simply isn't possible for even the most accomplished professional writer to go from draft to print, so don't try it. Your pride of authorship will blind you to blemishes you can't afford to miss.

You need some distance from your creative efforts to give yourself detachment and objectivity. There is no hard-and-fast rule about how long it should take to come up with the finished product; if you think you have finished, leave it alone, at least overnight. Then come back to it fresh. You'll read it almost as if it were meeting your eyes for the first time.

Before you email or print your letters, make sure that your writing is as clear as possible. Three things guaranteed to annoy cover letter readers are incorrect spelling, poor grammar, and improper syntax. Go back and check all these areas. If you think syntax has something to do with the IRS, you'd better get a third party involved; we have affordable proofreading services at www.knockemdead.com.

Chapter 8

USE COVER LETTERS TO GET FOUR TIMES THE INTERVIEWS

Great cover, broadcast, and follow-up letters won't get you a job if they sit on your desk like rare manuscripts. You have to do something with them.

In *Knock 'em Dead: The Ultimate Job Search Guide*, I spend more than 150 pages showing you the best ways to execute a job search, including a dozen different networking strategies. I'm going to dip into just a few tactics from that book to show you some of the ways to find names and titles of hiring authorities so that you can contact them directly.

Responding to job postings is a big part of most job searches, so while there are many other effective job search strategies, this chapter will focus on tactics that can double, triple, and quadruple your chances of getting interviews from job postings by identifying and approaching the people most likely to be in a position to hire you.

Online Job Postings

Whenever you see a job you can do, respond to the posting in the requested way. In addition, compile all contact information for the company, including website and mailing address. Whenever you can find the names and titles of managers likely to hold authority over the ultimate hiring decision (I'll show you how), you can approach them directly in three different ways, each approach increasing your chances of getting an interview:

1. Email your resume directly to that manager with a personalized cover letter, doubling your chances of an interview.

2. Send a resume and personalized cover letter by traditional mail to that manager, tripling your chances of an interview.

3. Make a follow-up telephone call to that manager first thing in the morning, at lunchtime, or at 5 P.M., quadrupling your chances of an interview.

How to Find Names of Hiring Authorities

The more frequently you speak with managers whose job titles signify that they have the authority to hire you, the faster you will land that new position. By approaching hiring managers directly, you skip waiting to have your resume pulled from a resume database, you sidestep the recruiter's evaluation process, and you have the attention of a hiring manager and can make a direct and personal pitch.

Your target for direct approach is always someone who can hire you, although any management title offers opportunity for referral. For example, while HR people won't have the authority to hire you, the pivotal nature of their work makes them aware of all areas within a company that could use your skills.

Getting a resume to the "right someone" by name and making a personalized pitch gives you a distinct advantage; this is never more important than when the economy is down or in recovery. At such times, your competition is fierce, and employers always recognize initiative and *motivation* as differentiating factors in your candidacy.

Who to Target in Your Job Search

I am going to tell you the hiring titles to target during your job search. As you read, make a list of the specific titles that apply in your professional world, because if you have a list of the high-value titles that specifically apply to your opening, you will be more likely to find the names that go with them.

1. Those titles most likely to be in a position to hire you are usually the management titles one, two, and three levels above you.

2. Other titles likely to have knowledge of an opening include:
   - Management titles 1–3 levels above you in departments that have ongoing interaction with your department.
   - Peers holding similar titles (a little less desirable).

3. Titles of people who are most likely to know those involved in the selection process, and are able to refer you. These titles might be employees of a target company, or employees of a company or organization that does business with such a company:

- Management titles 1–3 levels above you in any department
- Internal recruiters and HR professionals

Any name is better than no name, and with the Internet at your fingertips, there are endless opportunities to identify the names of people who carry the appropriate hiring titles for your needs.

Internet Research Tactics for Finding Names

With a little work you can find the names, titles, and contact information for a lot of the people who have the ultimate authority to hire someone like you. I'm going to start you on the right road in this chapter, but for a thorough guide on how to do this, study the job search chapters in the first 150 pages of the latest edition of *Knock 'em Dead: The Ultimate Job Search Guide*.

For a start, try keyword searches for your target hiring titles on Google, Bing, and other search engines. They are all likely to deliver names, and they'll all get different results.

For example, a professional in pharmaceutical sales looking to make direct contact with potential hiring authorities for a job at a specific company in the Pittsburgh area could try all the following keyword searches and gather new usable information on each search:

- Pharmaceutical sales (company name)
- Pharmaceutical sales (company name) Pennsylvania
- Pharmaceutical sales (company name) Pittsburgh
- Pharmaceutical Mgr sales (company name) Pennsylvania
- Pharmaceutical Mgr sales (company name) Pittsburgh
- Pharmaceutical Director sales (company name) Pennsylvania
- Pharmaceutical Director sales (company name) Pittsburgh
- Pharmaceutical VP sales (company name) Pennsylvania

Now take these additional steps:

- Repeat all without "pharmaceutical"
- Repeat all without company name
- Repeat with just the job title
- Repeat with separate searches for target title plus: hired, resigned, or deceased

Drill down, and you will come up with people holding these titles at this and other target companies in your area.

USE GOOGLE NEWS

When you have completed each of these searches first as a standard Google search, redo each one as a Google News search; this looks for mentions of your keywords in media coverage. Click on "News" above the standard Google search box.

When you do a Google News search for news about a company or a title within a company and find relevant intelligence, you can use it as an opener for your cover letter. Refer to the article and its relevance in your letter. Then copy and paste a URL to the reference if you're sending email, or enclose a copy of it with a traditional letter.

Try all the keyword combinations of job title, profession, location, and company phrases. You will come up with more job openings and job sites with most of them. When you drill down beyond the first couple of pages of results, you will come up with names to go with your target hiring titles for both your target company and for other companies.

Also check out the following resources:

- *Company websites.* On the "about us" pages, you can find names and sometimes contact information for management titles.
- *Biographical Directory/Database.* This is maintained by Standard & Poor's. It's a database of executives by name and title with contact information. Higher-level target hiring titles will be identifiable here or through one of the following options.

The following online resources are also useful for compiling a list of contacts to whom you can send your letter and resume:

- www.onesource.com/businessbrowserus.aspx
- www.knowx.com: Lists company owners, officers, and affiliations. Find out almost anything for about $60 a month.
- www.jigsaw.com: An extensive database of contact information. It charges $1 a name, but give them two names they don't have and you get credited a dollar.
- www.business.com/directory/advertising_and_marketing/sales/selling_techniques/lead_generation/: This page has links for lead-generation tools.

Names and Titles Increase Your Options

Sometimes, to alert all the right people at a target company that you're available, you might approach half a dozen different managers. For example, let's say you are a young engineer crazy for a job with Last Chance Electronics. It is well within the bounds of reason that you would submit a cover letter and resume to any or all of the following people, with each letter addressed by name to minimize its chances of going straight into the trash:

- Company president
- Vice president of engineering
- Chief engineer
- Engineering design manager
- Vice president of Human Resources
- Technical engineering recruitment manager
- Technical recruiter

Think through all the titles likely to be of use to you based on the above criteria, and keep all these titles in mind when you go looking for names to attach to them: The more options you have, the more results you will get.

Networking

One of the best ways to find names and get introductions to hiring authorities is to talk to people. *And because speaking with the people who can actually offer you a job is the only way you are going to get hired, the more ways you have to get into these conversations, the more successful you are going to be.*

When they are integrated into your job search, networking strategies deliver incredible results. Here are some effective ways to build relevant professional networks almost instantly.

Social Networking

Social networking has now become an integral part of cutting-edge job search and career-management strategies. It revolves around social and/or professionally oriented online networks that help you reach out to people you know, once knew, or would like to know. You can leverage your professional reach through connecting with others in your field, as well as through people with whom you share common experiences or interests.

Here's an example: A soldier who was cycling out of the military sought my help in her search for a new civilian career. First, to find other individuals with a similar background, I plugged in the word *army* at www.linkedin.com, perhaps the premier professional online networking site. I got more than 4,000 profiles of people who shared her military experience. (That was six years ago; with the same search today, I got 539,000: This growing connectivity is a big argument for joining LinkedIn.) We then tried a search using the phrase "*information technology*" (for her desired career change) and got 39,000 profiles (today it is well over one million). Both these potential networks would have relevance to her job search, but it got even better when we combined both the keywords: "*information technology* and *army*." This pulled up 908 profiles (today over 26,000) of people who shared her life experience and who had already made the transition into her desired profession. Such a degree of initial connectivity ensured she could hold helpful conversations with an enormous number of people, each of whom is relevant to her job search.

Corporate recruiters and headhunters often visit social networking sites, so you should shape the information you make available about yourself. For the professional in a job search, this will start with your resume (simply cutting and pasting your resume into your official profile) and possibly end there too. You make yourself visible, but because this is a social networking site and not a resume bank, you do it without an "I'm for sale" sign, which is useful when you are employed and looking for a new position.

HOW MANY SOCIAL NETWORKS ARE THERE?

There are just too many social networks to list, and the more these sites proliferate, the more specialized they become. It is probably a good idea to have a presence on two of the biggest, LinkedIn and Facebook. Beyond this, go to www.wikipedia.org and key in "social networks" for a complete listing. You'll find networking sites by special interests, languages, sex, race, and more.

Social networking can get you useful introductions to people throughout your profession, the country, and the world—people who might know of jobs at their own companies or who can introduce you to people at companies that have openings. This new application of technology enables you to reach out into an almost limitless community of like-minded professionals.

It works simply: You join a social networking site and find people you have worked with in the past. Then expand your network by joining the discussion groups that exist on all social networking sites and connect with other members of those groups.

For employers and recruiters, networking sites constitute a reliable pathway for recruiting qualified candidates, while for a job hunter they constitute a reliable pathway to jobs through the people connected to them. You can search a site's database by zip code, job title, company, or any keywords of your choice. The database will pull up the profiles of people who match your requirements and allow you to initiate contact directly, through your common membership in groups, or through the chain of people who connect you.

CAN SOCIAL NETWORKING HELP CAREER TRANSITION?

You will find social networking sites especially important when you are involved with or are planning a career transition. If you know you are cycling out of one profession and into another, you can use social networking sites to build a network of people who do the target job in your chosen profession and, whenever possible, people who have made a similar transition. If you are involved in a job search that involves career change, go to www.knockemdead.com and read the "Stepping Stones" article.

Professional Associations

One of the best things you can do for this job search and your long-term career success is to become an active member of one or two professional associations. You'll get job leads and an awesome network immediately, and such organizations provide great vehicles for increasing your credibility and visibility in the profession. In fact, if you have heard disgruntled job hunters mutter, "It's not what you know, it's who you know," it probably means they don't understand networking, and are probably not members of a professional association.

Associations have monthly meetings in most major metropolitan areas, plus regional and national get-togethers every year. The local meetings are of immediate interest, and unless you work on a national level, membership in the local or state chapters of a national association will be quite adequate for your needs—and cheaper, too. When you join a local chapter of a recognized national association and attend the local meetings, you get to know and be known by the most committed and best-connected people in your profession within your target marketplace. Your membership will help you stay attuned to what is going on in your profession, as associations offer ongoing training that makes you a more knowledgeable and therefore a more desirable employee.

The professional association is a new "old boy/old girl" network for the modern world. Your membership becomes a link to millions of colleagues, almost all of whom will gladly talk to you, based on your mutual connectivity through the association.

All industries and professions have multiple associations, any of which could be valuable depending on your needs. For example, if you are in retail, you could join any of some thirty national associations and fifty state associations. Together these associations represent employees of more than 1.5 million retail organizations, which in turn provide employment for more than 14 million people. Most other associations offer similarly impressive networking potential.

If you fit the profile of a special-interest or minority group, you will also find professional associations that cater to another dimension of the *professional you*. These include—but are by no means restricted to—associations for African Americans, Latinos, Asian Americans, professionals with disabilities, and women. If you can find a niche association that's a fit, join it: It represents another, even more finely tuned network.

A good place to start online is the Wikipedia professional associations page, or the library, where you can check out the *Encyclopedia of Associations* (published by Gale). Alternatively, you can try a Google search for relevant keywords. For example, "legal association" will generate listings of associations for the legal profession.

LOOK FOR NICHE ASSOCIATIONS

If you belong to any identifiable minority, use that in your Google searches as well. For example, "Asian legal association" will generate a listing of local associations for Asian professionals working in the legal field. When you join an association, you'll benefit greatly from attending the meetings, because this is where you will meet other professionals in your field. But don't just attend the meetings; get involved. Associations are largely volunteer organizations and always need someone to set out chairs or hand out paperwork and name tags. The task itself doesn't matter, but your visible willingness to be an active participant most certainly does, and will get you on a first-name basis with people you would probably never meet otherwise. Given the nature of association membership, you don't have to go straight from introductions to asking for leads on jobs. In fact, it can be productive to have initial conversations where you do not ask for leads or help in your job search, but where you make a contribution to the group; this is always preferable, because others are more likely to help you when they see you making an effort toward the common good.

It is easier to get to know people than you might think, because all professional association members are there, at least in part, to advance their careers through networking. Once you have the lay of the land, volunteer for one of the many committees that keep associations running. It's the best way to meet people and expand your sphere of influence, as you can reach out to others as you engage in your volunteer association activities. Committee involvement doesn't take much time because they invariably employ the "many hands make light work" approach; they are structured to function with the help of full-time professionals like you, with mortgages to pay and families to support.

There is a good argument that, from a networking point of view, the bigger the committee, the better. Membership and program committees are among the best to join. However, involvement in any committee will serve your needs, because being on one will enable you to reach out to those on other committees. If you join the conference or event committee, you can initiate contact with just about anyone in your professional world: "Hi, Bill Parsons? I'm Becky Lemon with the conference committee of the local association. I'd like to invite you to a meeting we are having next week on . . ."

Don't join committees for which you lack the experience to be a productive member, unless you make it clear that the reason you want to become a part of that team is for professional development—if this is the case, expect to become the designated water carrier, at least initially.

If you volunteer and become active in an association, the people with whom you come into contact will begin to identify you as a team player, and this perception can be instrumental in landing that new job and surging ahead in your career.

Use the Association Database or Directory

The association directory, which comes with your membership package, provides you with a superb networking resource for telephone and email networking campaigns. You can feel comfortable calling any other member on the phone and introducing yourself: "Hi, Brenda Massie? My name is Martin Yate. We haven't spoken before, but we are both members of the Teachers' Federation. I need some advice; can you spare a minute?"

Your mutual membership, and the commitment to your profession that it bespeaks, will guarantee you a few moments of anyone's time, a courtesy you should always return.

You can also use your association membership directory to generate personal introductions for jobs you have heard about elsewhere. For example, you might have found an interesting job posting on www.careerbuilder.com, or perhaps on a company website, with the request that you upload your resume. This is where your networking can pay big dividends. Apply just as the website where you found the job requested, then return to your membership directory and find people who work for that company. A judicious call or two will frequently get you a personal referral and some inside information on the opening: You have just *doubled your chances of landing that interview.* Once you have an interview scheduled, these same contacts can help you prepare for the interview with insider knowledge about the company, the department, and the hiring manager.

Professional associations all have online newsletters, and many have a jobs section on the website linked to the newsletter, where companies advertise because of the always qualified response. So you will see job postings here that often don't appear anywhere else. In down economic times, a savvy corporate recruiter will use an association website to skim the cream of available talent while screening out the less committed. You will also notice that association members write all the articles in the newsletters; as everyone likes to have their literary efforts appreciated, telling a member you have read an article that he has written gives you a great introduction to a networking call or letter.

Active association membership puts you on the radar of all the best qualified and best connected professionals in your area. You can also list it at the end of your resume under a Professional Affiliations heading. This is guaranteed to get a second glance, as it signifies professional awareness. Employers and headhunters will sometimes use words like *association*, *club*, and *society* in their keyword searches, so association membership will also help get your resume pulled up from the databases for investigation by human eyes.

How to Make Networking Work

Professional associations are just one of a dozen approaches to networking, all of which can be tremendously beneficial to your job search and overall career success if you nurture them.

Think of networking as professional connectedness, because becoming properly connected to your profession is the activity that will generate the widest range of relevant contacts for your job search.

You may well discover that your network is not as comprehensive as you might have wished, and that to be effective, your networking requires more than shooting the breeze with old cronies on the telephone. A successful outcome demands you move beyond the comfort level of inadequate personal networks.

Besides, just because you worked with someone five years ago doesn't mean she still regards you as a friend, especially if you haven't spoken to her since then. Surveys show that we all respond in these understandable ways:

- *To those requests from people I didn't know,* I asked for a resume (of course, if they had an introduction or were fellow members of an association, things would be different). If I received it in good time with a thoughtfully pre-pared accompanying letter, I would give that person help if I could.

- *To those requests from people with an introduction from someone I liked* and respected, I gave time and consideration and, whenever possible, assistance.
- *To those requests from friends, people I had worked with at one time* and who had kept in touch since we had worked together, I provided leads and even made calls on their behalf.
- *To those requests from people who regarded themselves as friends* but who had not maintained contact, or who had only re-established contact when they wanted something, for some reason I was unable to really help. I wished them the best of luck. "Sorry I couldn't help you. If something comes to mind, I'll be sure to call."

Nothing works like a personal recommendation from a professional colleague—and you get that by being a colleague, by being connected to your profession and the professionals within it, *and by being known as someone who cares and who shares*. It is no accident that successful people in all fields know each other; they helped each other become successful because they stayed in touch, through good times and bad, and helped each other whenever they could.

If you are going to use business colleagues and personal friends in your job search, don't mess up and do it halfheartedly. We live in a mobile society, so in addition to family, friends, and the colleagues you naturally know, it is *a smart long-term career-management strategy to establish yourself as a member of your professional community*.

A Very Smart Networking Idea

Intelligent networking encourages you to form relationships with people in your profession and industry at many levels. Almost anyone in your industry or location can be useful regardless of title or experience, but the people of most interest will likely fall into these categories:

1. Those who are 1–3 title levels above you and who might hire you, now or in the future. With this group, you can initiate contact by sending an email to introduce yourself and ask them to look at your profile. If this proceeds to a conversation and interviews, fine; if not, you can ask your contact to connect you to others.
2. Those at or below your level but with similar professional experience.
3. Those who work in related areas within the same profession or industry.

It's best to build a relationship by finding common ground. You can initiate relation-ships by asking for advice; many people will give you a few minutes of their time. You will develop the best relationships, though, by reaching out to others with help and advice, because when you offer good things, forging a relationship with you becomes important to the other person. It is easy to do this by taking an active part in special-interest groups and searching the social sites for people in your profession who are actively looking for jobs.

The challenge then becomes how to help, advise, or make a gesture that will encourage a relationship that shares introductions and job leads. The answer is logical and painless: Use the job leads you hear about that are inappropriate for your own use.

It's a not-so-funny thing about the job search: When you are fresh out of school, no one is hiring entry-level workers; they all want you to call back in five years. Five years later, when you are once again looking for a job, they now only want someone fresh out of school or with ten years' experience.

In your job search activities, you are constantly coming across positions that aren't right for you, but that could be just what someone else is aching to hear about. Offer these leads to others as part of your introduction. Here's how it can work: Sometimes you have to send an email stating why you want to make contact, and sometimes you can communicate immediately—it depends on a number of variables. In the first instance, you send an email simply stating that you have a job lead that the contact might find interesting. This is a nice gesture and will get you lots of introductions.

In the second instance, where you are actually in direct email communication, state your business: "I am involved in a strategic career move right now, and I have come across a job that isn't right for me, but that could be perfect for you. If you'd like to talk, let's exchange telephone numbers. I'll be happy to pass the lead on, and perhaps you have heard about something that would suit me . . . I am cycling out of the army and into the private sector and have been looking for jobs in IT in the South . . ."

DON'T TALK ABOUT YOUR IDEAL JOB

If you are serious about getting back to work quickly, never talk about what you want in that ideal next job when you are networking. It reduces the odds of someone telling you about an opening. Instead, talk about what you can do.

Your job search has you scouring the job sites for job leads, and now you have a use for all those positions that aren't quite right for you. Build your own database of the jobs that are not suitable for you and pass them on to all those people above and below you in your profession who will make perfectly symbiotic networking partners.

How Social Networks Expand Your Approach Options

When you find suitable job postings, you are usually faced with uploading your resume into a corporate or headhunter database, but now, along with your professional association memberships, social networks give you additional approaches.

On your social networking sites, look for people who work at that target company now or have in the past. Search for them, using the target company name in your keyword search, then look for job titles one, two, and three levels above your own, and then those at the same level or one or two beneath you.

NETWORKING AND GROUP DISCUSSION POSTS

All the social networking sites—LinkedIn, Facebook, etc.—have special-interest groups that are used by recruiters (be sure to connect with me). It is becoming increasingly common for job hunters to post pitches about themselves in the discussion groups. This helps you become visible to recruiters. This is done very effectively with the Subject Line technique we discussed in Chapter 7. At 133 characters, this subject line does double duty as a "signature resume" for group discussions:

Reg HR Manager—EEOC, FLSA, ADA, OSHA. 10 years' exp includes arbitration, campus, executive recruitment, selection, compensation, T&D

The more you reach out, the better your reputation becomes and the more others will reach out to you. You will find much more on social and other networking approaches in the latest edition of *Knock 'em Dead: The Ultimate Job Search Guide.*

Networking Letters

When you write networking emails and letters, use these guidelines for your structure; you can also use the same guidelines as frameworks for networking conversations:

1. Establish connectivity: something or someone in common, or information likely to be of interest.
2. Use your common membership in professional associations as a bridge builder to other members.
3. Let contacts know what you can do. They will invariably want to help, but you have to give them a framework within which to target their efforts. DO NOT tell them about your dream job, or the promotion you always hoped for; don't get

too specific, or allow your ego to get in the way of leads for jobs you really could do. You want to be specifically vague: "I'm looking for something in operations within the medical devices area" gives the listener the widest possible opportunity for coming up with leads.

4. Tell whomever you are writing or calling, "It's time for me to make a move" or "My job just got sent to Mumbai, and I'm hoping I could pick your brain."

5. Don't ask specifically, "Can you hire me?" or "Can your company hire me?" Ask for advice and leads. Then ask for guidance: "Could I send you my resume?"

6. By all means, ask for leads within specific target companies, but don't rely on a contact with a particular company to get you in.

7. When you do get help, say thank you. And if you get the help verbally, follow it up with a thank-you note in writing. The impression is indelible, and it just might get you another lead.

When you write networking letters and make the follow-up calls, you might be surprised to find who your friends are: Someone you always regarded as a real pal won't give you the time of day, and someone you never thought of as a friend will go above and beyond the call of duty on your behalf.

More on Referrals

Most people have horribly inadequate networks. The professional association strategy is just one of a dozen approaches you can learn to begin building and expanding them. You can learn much more about networking for referrals, finding names and titles of hiring authorities, making verbal presentations, recognizing and responding to "buy signals," and overcoming objections in the latest edition of *Knock 'em Dead: The Ultimate Job Search Guide.*

GET A FREE RESUME REVIEW FROM MARTIN YATE!
Go to the website of the store where you bought the book, write an honest review,
and send the link with your resume to *MartinYate@KnockEmDead.com.*

Chapter 9
SENDING OUT COVER LETTERS

A successful job search needs an integrated overall plan that includes all the most practical job search strategies.

On a call-in radio show during this last recession, I took a call from a woman who had "done everything and still not gotten a job." She explained that she had sent out almost 300 letters and still wasn't employed. After I asked her a couple of questions, I learned that she had been job-hunting for almost two years and had responded to two or three job postings a week. When I asked, she told me that as an accountant, there were probably some 2,000 companies for whom she could work. This means she was engaged in a job search that used only one largely passive approach to finding a job (responding to job postings) when there are at least five practical ways to find jobs, and where she only managed to approach about 15 percent of her customers in two years. Two employer contacts per week will not get you back to work—or even on the right track with the kind of job that can help you advance toward your chosen work-life goals.

Just sending out letters and resumes in response to job postings, without integrating them into more productive job search approaches, is a sad excuse for a job campaign. Email and traditional mail initiatives should be integrated into every aspect of your job search. They should be a vital part of your job search strategy. You will then need to maintain a balance among the *number* of emails and letters you send out on a daily and weekly basis, the *types* of emails and letters you send out, and how you follow up on them by making telephone calls to initiate the conversations that must take place to win job offers.

A Plan for a Direct Approach to Hiring Authorities

A professionally conducted campaign will include the ongoing identification of the names that go with "most-likely-to-hire" target job titles at target employers and use both email and traditional mail for initial approach, and then follow up with a phone call. This approach really works; you'll find step-by-step tactics laid out in the latest edition of *Knock 'em Dead: The Ultimate Job Search Guide*.

As you discover names to go with the priority job titles, send a personalized cover letter and resume via email and traditional mail and schedule a follow-up telephone call in your week's agenda.

Subsequently, send further resumes and personalized cover letters through email and traditional mail as you come up with the names of people who hold other "most-likely-to-hire" target job titles within that company. You might also consider book-marking desirable companies so you can regularly check in on their job openings.

This Is Not Your Last Job Search

This is probably not the first or the last job search you will ever do, so save all your job search letters within a career-management folder where you can find them again when you need them.

Develop electronic documents or paper file folders containing all the relevant information for each company. You'll want to keep the company's website and a list that includes the names of the company's executives and all other management names and titles that you have identified as relevant to your job search. Whenever you find other interesting information, copy it into the company folder. For instance, you might come across information on growth or shrinkage in a particular area of a company, or you might read about recent acquisitions the company has made; you can use the website, Google, and Google News to track these company activities.

All this information will help you target potential employers and stand out in different ways. Your knowledge will create a favorable impression when you first contact the company: That you made an effort is noticed and sets you apart from other applicants who don't bother. The combination says that you respect the company, the opportunity, and the interviewer; combined, these perceptions help differentiate your candidacy.

All your efforts have an obvious short-term value in helping you generate job interviews and offers. Whom would *you* interview and subsequently hire? The person who knows nothing about your company, or the person who knows everything and shows enthusiasm with that knowledge?

Your efforts also have long-term value, because you are building a personalized reference library of your target industry/specialty/profession that will get you off to a running start the next time you wish to make a job change.

Following Up: A Cautionary Tale

Although you will get calls from your mailing, if you sit there like Buddha waiting for the world to beat a path to your door, you might wait a long time.

A pal of mine placed a posting for an analyst. Within a week, he had received more than 100 responses. Ten days later, he'd received 50 more and was still plowing through them when he received a follow-up call (the *only* one he received) from one of the candidates who'd tracked down his name. The candidate's resume was "in the tank" with all the others, but the follow-up phone call got it discovered. The job hunter was in the office by the end of the day and returned the following morning, and she was hired by lunchtime. This is not an isolated incident: Candidates who make themselves visible get hired.

MAKE IT EASY FOR THE HIRING MANAGER

If you are not already successful in management, you need to know one of the success principles outlined in my book for managers titled *Hiring the Best*: "The first tenet of management is getting work done through others." Managers are always on the lookout for competent professionals in their field for today and tomorrow. BUT, they hate recruiting and interviewing; they just want to find the right person, hire her, and get back to work. All you have to do is help them by packaging yourself professionally and using the strategies and tactics learned in this book to make them aware of your existence.

Follow-Up Calls Work!

You'll notice that examples in the following letter section mention that the applicant will follow up with a phone call. This allows the writer to explain to any inquisitive receptionist that Joe Schmoe is "expecting my call" or that it is "personal," or, "it's accounting/engineering/customer service business."

It's surprising that so many people are nervous about calling a fellow professional on the phone and talking about what they do for a living. *Don't worry so much.* In this unsettled world there is an unwritten credo shared by the vast majority of professional people: You should always help one another if it isn't going to hurt you in the process. Everyone out there has been in your situation and knows it can happen at any moment. Because of this, almost everyone you speak to will be sympathetic to your cause and help you if they can and, of course, if you ask the right questions.

No manager will take offense at a call from a professional colleague, and this is what you are. To know exactly how to make the call and what to say, look at the chapters on making contact and telephone interview in the latest edition of *Knock 'em Dead: The Ultimate Job Search Guide*.

Use a Contact Tracker

To ensure that you keep track of your mailings and the follow-up phone calls, I recommend that you create a Contact Tracker on a spreadsheet program like Microsoft Excel. Create columns for the company name, telephone number, email address, and contact name. As a rule of thumb, an email sent today is ripe for follow-up within twenty-four to forty-eight hours; a mailing sent today is ripe for follow-up three to five days later.

Cover Letters: The Key to Your Job Search

Nine out of ten hiring managers prefer a cover letter with a resume, so a great cover letter will guarantee your resume gets read with serious attention. It will set you apart from other candidates and increase your interviews. You'll even have more productive and successful interviews, because the hiring manager will have a better idea of who you are professionally and who you are as a person.

The sample section that follows includes many types of job search letters that you can use throughout your search to help your candidacy stand out. Hope to see you soon at www.knockemdead.com, and join me every day on the Secrets & Strategies group on LinkedIn for more discussion and live workshops.

GET A FREE RESUME REVIEW FROM MARTIN YATE!
Go to the website of the store where you bought the book, write an honest review, and send the link with your resume to *MartinYate@KnockEmDead.com*.

Chapter 10
SAMPLE LETTERS

Here's the real meat and potatoes of the book—the sample letters you can use as models for your own.

Apart from the sender's name and address (the personal stationery aspect), all letters adhere to Houghton Mifflin's *Best Writer's Guide* specifications. To those who might notice these things, it is important that we present an impeccable attention to detail.

COVER LETTERS FOR DIFFERENT PROFESSIONS

Accounting Manager

To:

From:

Cc:

Subject: Accounting Manager job posting

Re: File No. 213

Dear [Name]:

I have six years of accounting experience and am responding to your recent posting for an Accounting Manager. Please allow me to highlight my skills as they relate to your stated requirements.

Your Requirements	My Experience
• A recognized accounting degree plus several years of practical experience.	• Obtained a CA degree in 2020 and have three-plus years' experience as an Accounting Manager.
• Excellent people skills and demonstrated ability to motivate staff.	• Effectively managed a staff of 18 including two supervisors.
• Strong administrative and analytical skills.	• Assisted in the development of a base reference library with Microsoft Excel for 800 clients.
• Good oral and written communication skills.	• Trained four new supervisors via daily coaching sessions, communication meetings, and technical skill sessions.

I believe my background provides the core professional skills you require. I would welcome the opportunity for a personal interview to further discuss my qualifications and have enclosed my resume for your consideration.

Yours truly,

[Your name]
[Your telephone number]

Accounting Manager

To:

From:

Cc:

Subject: Accounting Manager Position

Re: [Job name and ref. number]

Dear [Name]:

I am writing to express my interest in and enthusiasm for the Accounting Manager position posted on [where it was found].
As an accounting manager, I am well versed in the full range of accounting functions sought by your company: A/R, A/P, P&L, payroll, and benefits administration. Because of my experience and expertise in these areas, I have the ability to make resolute, well-informed decisions about accounting issues. I am research and detail oriented, analytical, and organized with exceptional time-management skills.

I constantly take the initiative in seeking out new responsibilities and challenges, and I take pride in nurturing pride and professional growth in all my reports, being patient with a professional demeanor and articulate communication style. As an accountant I am diligent in all I do and instill this in my team.

I have attached a resume that will put my skills and experience in context for you. I would welcome the opportunity to meet with you to discuss how I can meet your needs and contribute to your team. Please call me at (709) 976-8764. If we haven't spoken before, I will call you next [insert day] to set up a meeting.

Sincerely,

[Your name]
[Your telephone number]

Administrative Investment Banker

To:
From:
Cc:

Subject: Administrative Investment Banker job posting
_____

Dear [Name]:

I am responding to the Administrative Investment Banker job posting on your company's website. My 12+ years' experience as an administrative investment banker and assistant to a Vice Chairman seems a good match for your stated needs.

Some things not mentioned in your posting that I know will be important considerations: In bank administration we do what needs to be done to keep the engine running smoothly. In addition to all your stated requirements, administration responds to the legal and political polemics that proscribe the banker's world. I have had a seat on the legal committee for 7 years, and spent 4 years as a PAC representative.

My years as a line and administrative professional have also provided me with an unusual sensitivity to the needs of senior professionals. I have substantial computer experience and am fully computer literate. I have been told my verbal and written communication skills are exceptional.

I know of your company, and my colleague _____ is a VP in the systems area; we tend to be happy in similar environments, so I would be eager to talk with you about this position.

Based on the responsibilities and opportunities you describe, and the industry norms for this job, you'll find my salary requirements reasonable and negotiable. I have attached my resume for your consideration in both MS Word and as a PDF. And as I'm a guy who likes to cover all bases, I also pasted an unformatted version after my signature.

Sincerely,

[Your name]
[Your telephone number]
Attachment: resume

Administrative Secretary

To:

From:

Cc:

Subject: I put out administrative fires

Dear [Name]:

I was excited to see the announcement for the Administrative Secretary position with the Fire Department, and believe I am an excellent candidate. After reading the job posting, I arranged for an informative tour from my uncle, James Kenderline, which confirmed my interest in the position.

Throughout my career I have demonstrated a strong work ethic as well as outstanding secretarial, administrative, reception, and records maintenance skills. I am meticulous with detail, can multitask effectively, and resolve problems in a fast-paced and deadline-driven environment. Among my professional accomplishments are:

- Concurrently handled full-time employment, managed rental properties, and completed my Bachelor of Science Degree in English and Writing, earning a 3.5 GPA.

- Assumed additional responsibilities proactively, and as requested, such as researching and authoring a well-received full-page article for a client newsletter—with only 4 hours' notice—when the EAP manager was unable to come up with fresh ideas.

- Contributed ideas that streamlined processes and optimized productivity.

Working for the Fire and Rescue Department would be an exciting and honorable position, and I think that upon reviewing my resume, you will find that my qualifications would be a great fit for this job.

I look forward to a personal meeting when we can discuss how my credentials and work ethic could contribute to your organization.

Sincerely,

[Your name]
[Your telephone number]
Attachment: resume

Assistant Director of Campus Housing

To:

From:

Cc:

Subject: Assistant Director of College Housing job posting

Re: Reference Code: TC-E-5556E2

Dear [Name],

In response to your posting on the NACE website for an Assistant Director of College Housing, I have attached my resume for your review. The following gives you a snapshot of how my experience matches your needs:

Your Requirements	My Qualifications
• Bachelor's degree or four years of experience in lieu of degree.	• Master's degree in Clinical Counseling. Eight years of combined experience in resident hall administration and counseling capacities.
• Promote and develop educational programming and maintain extensive budget.	• Plan, develop, and implement educational programs, and manage an operational budget.
• Administration of three to five residence halls housing approximately 1,000 students.	• Administration of residence halls housing up to 500 college students.
• Supervise, develop, and evaluate three to five full-time resident hall directors.	• Supervise, develop, and evaluate 26 Resident Advisors with direct responsibility for four RAs and a Head Resident Advisor (HRA).
• Develop departmental policies and procedures, manage area office including billing, occupancy, and facilities records.	• Direct all aspects of front desk management and facilities maintenance operations.
• Assist in the development and leadership of departmental committees, and serve as manager for student conduct cases.	• One year as VP of Committees and Organizations for the Student Government with the State University of New York at Suffolk.

Thank you for your review and consideration of my attached resume. I look forward to hearing from you soon.

Sincerely,

(555) 555-1234

Executive Assistant Referral

To:

From:

Cc:

Subject: Executive Assistant referral

Dear [Name],

I was very pleased to learn of the need for an Executive Assistant in your company from your colleague [name]. I believe the qualities you seek are well matched by my track record:

Your Needs	My Qualifications
Independent Self-Starter	• Served as company liaison between sales representatives, controlling commission and products.
	• Controlled cash flow, budget planning, and bank reconciliation for three companies.
Computer Experience	• Utilized QuickBooks in preparing financial spreadsheets used in private placement memoranda.
	• Have vast experience with both computer programming and all current office management software and communications protocols.
Compatible Background	• Served as an executive assistant to four corporate heads.

A resume is attached that covers my experience and qualifications in greater detail. I would appreciate the opportunity to discuss my credentials in a personal interview.

Sincerely,

(555) 555-1234
Attachment: resume

Entry-Level Business Analyst

To:

From:

Cc:

Subject: Entry-Level Business Analyst

Dear [Name],

It was a pleasure to meet members of your team at the career fair yesterday. I have the skills for and would like to formally apply for the Entry-level Business Analyst position. I am currently a fourth-year undergraduate and will earn my Bachelor of Management degree in April 2018.

I have worked my way through school with full-time jobs for the past four years, so I have real experience in the professional world and I'm eager to get my career started.

I have excelled in my professional experiences, including sales, project management, customer service, and group projects. I am a thorough team player with strong analytical, organizational, and time-management skills. I believe my skills paired with my enthusiasm to learn are qualities that you are looking for in the successful candidate who joins your team.

With knowledge and interest in your company, practical experience with the skills you require, and commitment to results, I want this opportunity. You are recruiting on campus for an entry-level position; where else will you find an entry-level Business Analyst with almost four years' professional experience?

I would appreciate the opportunity for a personal interview. My resume is attached, and my telephone number is below. Thank you in advance for your time and consideration.

Sincerely,

(555) 555-1234

Mike Shrezski

Broadhurst, NY 11573

(555) 555-1990
516accountant@hotmail.com

[Date]

Name
[Title]
Company Name
Address
Address

Dear [Name]:

I am writing in response to your posting for a [title of position] on [where you found the ad]. My professional experience will make me an excellent choice for [title of position], plus my recent degree ensures that I have the latest training and academic credentials.

I offer:
- A solid educational foundation in accounting and finance.
- Management and employee training skills to improve organizational performance.
- A proven ability to work with individuals from diverse cultural and socioeconomic backgrounds.
- A solid track record of excellent academic and workplace performance.

I have enclosed my resume for your review, which will give you an idea of my educational qualifications and work experience. I look forward to the opportunity to meet with you and further discuss how I might contribute as a member of your team. I can be reached at (555) 555-1990 or 516accountant@hotmail.com. Thanks for your time and consideration.

Sincerely,

Mike Shrezski
Attachment: resume

Finance

To:

From:

Cc:

Subject: (Job name and ref. number)

Dear [Name]:

I am writing to express my interest for the [title] position, posted [insert where found]. I offer more than four years' hands-on experience with financial, accounting, and benefits services for government agencies with a degree in Economics. I have secret clearance and DOD, IAA, PII, Privacy Act, and HIPAA Operations Certifications.
As a financial services professional, my experience includes:

- ✓ Implementing policy and procedural guidelines, making adjudication decisions, and executing processes following specified instructions.
- ✓ Investigating and resolving customer issues related to recoupments, exemptions, and payment issues.
- ✓ Evaluation and processing payments in accordance with the Prompt Payment Act.
- ✓ Tracking ACES program costs and quality through the GoNavy Ed database.
- ✓ Examination of invoices for discrepancies and confirmation of accuracy.

I have a strong work ethic, a commitment to personal and departmental success, and I strive to deliver consistently error-free work. I learn quickly, thrive on challenges, I'm flexible in adapting to new environments, and I am always willing to go the extra mile no matter what the task.

I have attached my resume for your review, and I look forward to discussing how my skills might fit your needs. I can be reached at (555) 555-8734.
Sincerely,

[Your name]
[Your telephone number]

Financial Analyst

To:

From:

Subject: Ben Solee said to contact you re Financial Analyst position

Dear [Name],

I recently spoke with our mutual friend Ben Solee, and he strongly recommended that I send you a copy of my resume. I am very pleased to learn of the need for a Finance Associate, and I believe the qualities you seek are well matched by my track record:

Your Needs	My Qualifications
3–5 years of experience building and maintaining complex financial models	• Four years of experience at a top-performing hedge fund
	• Built and maintained complex financial models to support investment in private equity transactions and coverage of over 30 stocks, $100M of portfolio value
	• Created matrices in Excel to analyze model sensitivity to risk factors
Background of exceptional academic performance	• BS in Economics with Honors from the California Institute of Technology (Caltech)
Ability to manage multiple projects and meet deadlines	• Delivered 15–20 research reports and notes per month in a fast-paced work environment

My greatest strength lies in my ability to clearly communicate complex financial information. This has enabled me to summarize the results of models and in-depth due diligence into concise investment theses for portfolio managers, which have resulted in profitable investments and avoided as many losers.

If rumors of the job are true, I hope to speak with you further and will call the week of August 2nd to follow up with you. Hopefully, you'll be so fired up by the attached resume, you'll call or email me sooner.

Sincerely,

[Your name]
[Your telephone number]

Heavy Equipment Supervisor

To:
From:
Cc:
Subject: Heavy Equipment Supervisor job posting

Dear [Name],

Please accept the attached resume in response to your Heavy Equipment Supervisor position posting.

My experience includes 10+ years of experience operating and maintaining heavy equipment. In my current position, I operate backhoes, loaders, Lulls, Galion cranes, Ditch Witch trenchers (large and walk-behind), forklifts, street sweepers, and bucket trucks. In addition, I supervise the troubleshooting, maintenance, and repair of all of the department's equipment.

Of equal importance are my supervisory and leadership skills; I have managed crews of up to 40 employees. Being extremely diligent, I have assumed responsibility for overseeing and monitoring various projects and issues that affect the daily operations, efficiency, and profitability of the company. I am recognized by senior management for consistently completing projects on time and within budget.

My transition through several trades during my career has developed my strong multi-tasking abilities, which have proven to be an asset in a business where everything needs to be done yesterday.

Assuming my skills match your needs, I would welcome the opportunity to meet with you and determine what contributions I can make to your company. Thank you for your consideration. My resume is attached for your review.

Sincerely,

(555) 555-1234

Hydrologist

To:

From:

Cc:

Subject: **Hydrogeologist/Groundwater Modeler:** solute transport modeling, quantitative skills

RE: Position of Hydrogeologist/Groundwater Modeler, Company Job ID: ACHZ4121-234059, AJB Reference Number: 4950495, Job ID #0000BZ/BBBB

Dear [Name]:

I learned about your need for a Hydrogeologist/Groundwater Modeler with great interest, as my qualifications match your requirements for this position almost exactly. Please accept my attached resume for your review and allow me to explain briefly how I can contribute to ____.

With an MS Degree in Hydrologic Sciences and over 7 years of research experience, I have developed a strong background in advanced theories of solute transport modeling; consequently, I have developed effective quantitative skills and a practical understanding of the fundamental principles and concepts associated with hydrogeology.

My resume will provide additional details regarding my educational background and professional experience. Beyond these qualifications, it may be helpful for you to know that I have worked successfully in both independent and team project environments, adapt readily to rapidly changing work conditions, and enjoy the prospect of contributing to CRPH's "80-year reputation as a water industry leader" in the advancement of hydrogeologic and groundwater projects.

I would welcome the opportunity to interview for this position and discuss the results you can expect from me as a member of your team. Thank you for your time and consideration.

My resume is attached for your review.

Sincerely,

(555) 555-1234

HR Management

To:

From:

Cc:

Subject: H.R. Management

Dear [Name],

I was excited to see your posting for an experienced H.R. Director with union experience because it so closely matches my skills.

With a primary focus on targeted recruiting, employee engagement, and skill development, my focus at work is to ensure that my employer has qualified staff, matched with the right positions, properly trained and consistently encouraged to pursue professional development—and so delivering that most valuable asset: skilled and motivated human resources.

A sample of my recent achievements includes:

- An open-door H.R. policy and visible efforts to improve employee programs/services that position H.R. as helpful to the individual.
- Successfully navigated a highly unionized environment, including negotiating with union representatives, dealing with employee grievances, and ensuring compliance with contracted terms. No walkouts, strikes, or threats of same in last five years.
- Establishing a productivity-oriented workforce through orientation, ongoing training, and educational programs.

I am a dependable and enthusiastic contributor with a profound sense of loyalty and commitment to finding solutions to complex situations. Given my research of your company I truly believe that I could quickly become an immediate and valuable contributor to your team.

Please contact me with any questions or to discuss the position in further detail. Thank you for your consideration.

Sincerely,

[Your name]
[Your telephone number]

Intern

To:

From:

Cc:

Subject: [Job name and ref. number]

Dear [Name]:

I have always had a passion for the fashion industry and I recently moved to New York to make this happen. I am enthusiastically applying for the Merchandising Internship recently posted [where]. I am a multilingual and multicultural professional with a background in organizational management and experience in design-to-manufacturing-to-market cycle. My professional skills are backed with the academic rigor of a law degree that gives me a degree of professional maturity beyond my years; that may be difficult to find in other candidates.

I will also bring experience in boutique design and interior decoration, plus a good grounding in fabrics. As a professional I always strive to create value, and in my experience to date have:

- Arranged advertising, marketing content, and strategically placed advertisements to attract desired target market.
- For a Swiss watchmaker, conceived and assisted in the prototype design for a line of women's watches.
- Scheduled client appointments, record management, and negotiations with vendors, and provided customer service excellence.
- Arranged onsite logistics for Relocation Department including transportation and accommodations for clients.
- Negotiated contract terms and managed all closing and follow-up services with clients.

I believe that I possess the ability and initiative to consistently deliver on my responsibilities as your next Merchandising Intern. I would be delighted to have the opportunity for a personal interview. Thank you in advance for your time and consideration.

Sincerely,

[Your name]
[Your telephone number]

International Management

To:

From:

Cc:

Subject: International Sales Manager referral

Re: International Sales Manager

Dear [Name]:

I was recently speaking with Hart Singh from your company and he strongly recommended that I send you a copy of my resume in reference to the above position. Knowing the requirements, he felt that I would be an ideal candidate. I have a BSc in electrical engineering and speak French and German.

For more than eleven years, I have been involved in international sales management, with seven years directly in the aerospace industry. My qualifications for the position include:

- ◆ Establishing sales offices in France, Great Britain, and Germany.
- ◆ Recruiting and managing a group of 24 international sales representatives.
- ◆ Providing training programs for all of the European staff, which included full briefing on our own products as well as competitor lines.
- ◆ Obtaining 42%, 33%, and 31% of the French, German, and British markets, respectively.
- ◆ Dealing with all local engine and airframe manufacturers.
- ◆ Generating more than $32 million in sales with excellent margins.

I feel confident that an interview, which would demonstrate my expertise in setting up rep organizations and training and managing an international sales department, could be time well spent. I look forward to meeting with you and will give you a call to follow up on this letter before the end of the week.

My resume is attached for your review.

Yours truly,

International Sales and Marketing

To:

From:

Cc:

Subject: International Consumer sales

Dear [Name],

I spoke with Jackson Pollock recently (he sends his best), and he felt my eight years' experience in international consumer sales, with intimate knowledge of your product line, would be of interest. He suggested contacting you.

I know your brand and as a sales professional, I appreciate the ease with which I can sell your product line, because as a woman, I appreciate the high standards of quality that define each product in your line.

My experience working with South American retailers gives me a good understanding of differing cultures and traditions, and my fluent Spanish helps.

My resume is attached, and if you have any questions I may be reached via this email address or at the number below. I would very much like to establish communication with you, and I will be calling you within the next few days.

Sincerely,

(555) 555-1234

Nonprofit Executive Director

Cherish Patowski

Possum Trot, Kentucky

934.432.4538

socialimpact934@yahoo.com

[Date]

[Selection Committee]
[Company Name]
[Mailing Address]
[City, State and Zip Code]

Dear [Selection Committee]:

As a seasoned Executive Director of large nonprofit organizations, I offer vast experience in all aspects of nonprofit management, including volunteer recruitment and training, collaboration with executive boards, strategic planning, public relations, and special events management. The following executive brief highlights how my background meets your stated position requirements.

You Require:	My Qualifications:
Resource development & fundraising expertise with a proven record of developing and implementing revenue-producing special events	• Experience planning marketing strategy and directing successful fundraising campaigns ranging from $.5 million to $200 million. • Demonstrated ability to increase fundraising by identifying, cultivating, and soliciting donors, including HNW and UHNW individuals and corporate partners.
Nonprofit management experience	• Over 16 years building cooperative and productive community business relationships. • Experience developing program, organizational, financial, and administrative plans with the board of directors of philanthropic organizations. • Strengths in recruiting, hiring, training, and motivating professional staff as well as promoting active and broad participation by volunteers.
Strategic planning & goal achievement	• Strategic vision and planning skills to help position organization for growth. • Ability to build collaborative relationships with the Board of Directors, business and community leaders, government officials, and not-for-profit organizations to craft strategic plans. • Exceptional organizational analysis abilities to identify organizational opportunities, and the strategies to move the organization forward. • Attention to keeping the Board of Directors informed of significant developments and trends in the field.
Financial management experience	• Experience developing and implementing sound financial practices to maintain the organization's financial integrity through proper recordkeeping and reporting to achieve annual financial objectives.
Skill in communications/publicity	• Ability to maintain a high public profile and act as a spokesperson and writer to communicate a compelling vision and build support for the organization's mission. • Proven talent for Public Relations initiatives to support organization's activities and events.

I would appreciate the opportunity to meet with you personally so that we may further discuss how my experience and leadership might serve the particular needs of your organization. I look forward to hearing from you and will contact you in a couple of days to arrange a time for us to meet.

Best regards,

Cherish Patowski

Attachment

Operations Director

To:

From:

Cc:

Subject: [Job name and ref. number]
_____

Dear [Name]:

As Director of Operations Services for the national restaurant chain Stuckey's, I am skilled in workforce development and total quality management. I am interested in your posted position for Director of Operations & Workforce Development.

Perhaps my greatest strength is developing franchise owners and general managers' ability to achieve higher productivity, profitability, and customer loyalty. However, it's a tough call because I also offer extensive experience and deliver demonstrated leadership with:

- New Restaurant Openings, Chain-Wide Restaurant Operations, & Facilities Management
- Budget Forecasting & Administration
- Vendor Sourcing & Negotiations for Cost Controls
- Crisis & Turnaround Management
- Technology Integration for Productivity & Process Optimization
- Employee Engagement, Employee Incentive Programs, & Performance Management

The attached resume illustrates the results I've achieved in situations common to all national franchisors. After you've had a chance to review, I would welcome a personal interview for the Director of Operations & Workforce Development opportunity. I look forward to what I anticipate will be the first of many positive communications. Thank you.

Sincerely,

[Your name]
[Your telephone number]

Operations Management

To:

From:

Cc:

Subject: Operations Management

___

Dear [Name]:

I am interested in, and qualified for the [insert title] position [insert where found] I am an engineering and operations professional with fifteen years of telecom experience, eight years of project management, and five years of management skills.

I have a demonstrated history of working with a wide range of rapid-paced, multi-site projects and programs. My day-to-day responsibilities include budget analysis, resource allocation, performance and project reviews, and managing the relationships between the company and the client.

Here are a couple of capabilities that I know you seek in operations management professionals:

- Operational leadership that has driven significant improvements to EBITDA.
- Productivity improvement allowing two data center closures and resulting in improved performance with less overhead.

As a director of operations, I understand the importance of clear communication between cross-functional teams, often including vendors, and bring to this work motivation and dedication to consistently delivering the desired outcomes on time and on budget. My management and leadership skills allow me to take pride in delivering complex projects and programs that increase shareholders' interests.

The attached resume will fill out details of my professional history and the above claims. Can we talk?

Sincerely,

(555) 555-1234

Paralegal

To:

From:

Cc:

Subject: Paralegal Position

Re: [Job name and ref. number]

Dear [Name]:

Your posting for a corporate paralegal [insert where found] indicated requirements that match my background and expertise. Throughout my seven-year paralegal career, I have maintained the highest performance standards with a diverse range of litigation functions. I am highly proficient and comfortable in the use of technology and use Westlaw and LexisNexis to perform research for the firm to assist in the management of complex cases.

I offer excellent organizational and communication skills, outstanding work ethic, and the ability to work well in both team-oriented and self-directed environments. I am able to deal with strict deadlines, assist in monitoring compliance with company-wide policies and procedures, while exercising discretion in all I do.

I would welcome an opportunity to meet with you to discuss my qualifications and candidacy in further detail. Please feel free to contact me at (555) 555-8266 or at the above email address. Thank you for your time and consideration.

Sincerely,

[Your name]
[Your telephone number]

Peace Officer

Dear [Name]:

I am submitting my attached resume in application for the position of Peace Officer. I have recently completed necessary educational requirements, and I am enthusiastic about the possibility of interviewing for this position.

My degree from _____ _____ in Criminal Studies provided me the opportunity to analyze the key concepts, principles, and practices associated with human behavior and criminal justice. I demonstrated in-depth knowledge of law enforcement and social science issues through excellent work in class assignments and projects.

I realize that there is a significant difference between academic studies and field experience, but I am confident that my knowledge and commitment to criminal justice will ensure my ability to perform effectively within your department.

I worked through college, earning recognition from my managers for my leadership and organizational skills. For example, as a Certified Trainer at _____, I trained a staff of eight bussers and contributed to improved team performance by building great relationships with team members and guests.

My resume is attached to provide you with full details concerning my background and achievements. Thank you for your time and consideration.

Sincerely,

(555) 555-1234

Program Management

To:

From:

Cc:

Subject: Question from IT Program Manager financial services

Dear [Name],

May I ask your advice and assistance?

As a result of a merger between my bank and another, I am exploring my opportunities. Although confident of a role in the new organization, I believe this is a perfect opportunity for making a strategic career move.

In my current role as an IT Program Manager, I have led the development of key financial systems and co-managed the seamless migration of two divisions to another state, delivering noteworthy cost savings and productivity gains. These and many other achievements are outlined in the attached resume.

As you will see, for the past eleven years, I've worked with blue-chip companies and have been entrusted with the direction of large-scale, global projects. This experience gives me a wide frame of reference and the ability to make informed decisions in a timely manner. I've implemented new systems, designed testing methods, managed resources, repaired damaged vendor relations, and put out all kinds of fires.

My career has accelerated based on the results, as you'll note from the accomplishments in my attached resume. I would appreciate a few minutes of your time to seek your advice. I'll phone you in a few days to see if we can schedule a brief meeting.

Thanks very much.

Regards,

[Your name]
[Your telephone number]
Attachment: resume

Radiologist

To:

From:

Cc:

Subject: [Job name and ref. number]

Dear [Name]:

Your recent posting for a Radiologic Technologist fits my qualifications, and I am writing to express my interest in the opportunity. I have been a Radiologic Technologist since 2011. I am an ARRT, LSRT, and I have obtained my BLS/CPR certification. My work ethic delivers excellent patient care, quality X-ray imaging, dependability, and flexibility.

I am accustomed to high-volume environments and can do weekend ER shifts when needed.

These experiences have prepared me to become a knowledgeable and competent technologist. I use my organizational skills to manage multiple priorities and I learn operational standards, policies, and procedures quickly.

My understanding and compassion toward others in difficult circumstances impacts everything I do in all circumstances. In a very real way, my customers always come first. My skills also include the often-overlooked ability to put patients at ease by explaining procedures and establishing a comfortable environment, which helps me consistently produce high-quality diagnostic film.

I would welcome the opportunity to meet and further discuss my qualifications as they relate to your needs. I have attached my resume and can be reached at the above email or by phone at (555) 555-6548.
Sincerely,

[Your name]

Research Associate

Susan Mackerley

Bad Axe, WV   (845) 901-0632   research914@gmail.com

June 30th, 2016

Venter Institute
Rockville, MD 20850

RE: Research Associate
Reference Code: INNE 2387

Dear [Name]:

I am responding to your job posting for a Research Associate I/II located on science.com. I have four years of in-depth experience in molecular biology techniques combined with a Master of Philosophy in Molecular Medicine and Pharmacology, and I would like to bring my skills to the Ventner Insitute.

As a research assistant my background includes hands-on experience of independently designing experiments, including establishing schedules, scope, and analyzing data while following appropriate protocols and exercising professional judgment.

As a research associate, I create value in a number of ways:

- Excellent organizational and time management skills with the ability to manage multiple projects simultaneously in fast-paced environments with changing requirements and priorities.
- Ability to operate laboratory equipment, including balances, centrifuges, speed vac, spectrophotometer, and autoclave while adhering to safety procedures and protocols.
- Maintain accurate and up-to-date laboratory records and biological stocks representing work performed.
- Maintain laboratory equipment, reagents, and inventory.

In addition to the above, I have the verbal and written communication skills to deliver technical presentations to diverse groups. I possess strong analytical and research skills, manage my time and priorities effectively and I work well independently and as part of cross-functional teams.

I would very much like to schedule a meeting where we can further discuss my qualifications to become part of your research team. May we meet to further discuss your needs?

Sincerely,

Susan Mackerley
(845) 901-0632
research914@gmail.com

Sales and Marketing

To:

From:

Cc:

Subject: Sales & Marketing Position

Dear [Name],

I am confident that I can help you meet the challenges outlined in your recent [where you found the ad, e.g., *Wall Street Journal*, Monster.Com, etc.] advertisement. Your job description speaks directly to my experience as a sales professional who is driven by success and fully understands the importance of developing winning strategies to achieve revenue goals.

As an intern, my energy and passion for my work made me exceptionally motivated, with a realistic understanding of what it is to work in highly demanding, self-starting environments. I have the skills you need, and I am ready to be challenged.

My eagerness to embrace new experiences gives you the versatility to place me in a number of contexts with confidence that the level of excellence you expect will be met. I am a persuasive communicator and perceptive listener with a strong work ethic and a highly approachable manner. I take pride in my customer-centered, service-imperative attitude and I have demonstrated success building and nurturing client relationships.

My resume is attached, and I am certain that a face-to-face meeting will fully reveal my ability to meet your expectations. Thank you for your time and consideration. I look forward to meeting with you.

Sincerely,

Françoise Garcia
847-268-9477

Sales and Marketing Manager

To:

From:

Cc:

Subject: Sales & Marketing Manager

Dear [Name]:

Your recent posting (Sales.com Job #45687) for a Sales & Marketing Manager mirrors all the skills I have developed over eighteen years.

I have had extensive exposure in leading sales and marketing operations. Some highlights and talents in these areas are:

- Generated new revenue by establishing referral partnerships with local and regional professional services firms.
- Improved overall business growth, driving revenue 300% and profit 270% over six years through development of strong client relationships and creating business outsourcing solutions for mid-sized corporate clients.
- Boosted sales of ancillary service products 93%, generating $3.1 million in additional revenue, increasing customer penetration and earning multiple company awards.

I consider myself a hands-on leader and motivator by example, adept at inspiring high-performance teams to deliver groundbreaking products in a highly competitive, ever-changing marketplace. Moreover, my well-developed verbal and written communication skills have forged the highest respect from clients as well as internal and external stakeholders.

With an ability that comes from years of hands-on experience, I can readily align my wide range of skills with strategic business development targets. I can guarantee considerable expertise in identifying opportunities, performing in-depth due diligence, and acting on viable initiatives to increase revenue.

The attached resume will give you further insight into my potential for making worthwhile contributions to your company. Thank you for your time and consideration. My number is below, and I am just a call away.

Sincerely,

(555) 555-1234

Sales Associate

To:

From:

Cc:

Subject: Sales Associate with verifiable track record

Dear [Name],

If you are you searching for a success-driven entry-level Sales Associate with a verifiable track record, look no further. Highlights of my achievements include:

- Paid college expenses while working full-time in sales.
- Awarded with three plaques and nominated to President's Club for exemplary sales performance.

Although I will not graduate with a BA in Communications until December, I am eager to start work as soon as possible—either full- or part-time. I can balance the responsibilities of a Sales Associate position with my final studies, because I have done so with a full course load for the past four years.

As a technology nut with proven closing ability in B-to-C sales, I am confident that I can make a positive contribution to your sales department. My resume is attached for your review. Unless I hear from you first, I will call you in a couple of days to arrange an interview. Thank you for your consideration.

Sincerely,

(555) 555-1234

Roslyn, NY 11567   **Mike Davis**   Phone (516) 843-9268
SupplychainNY@gmail.com

[Month, Day], 2017

[Name]
[Company Name]
[Address]
[City, State Zip]

Reference: [Job Title]

Dear [Name],

I am a performance-focused Supply Chain Leader with twenty years' experience with a history of accelerating growth to achieve world-class status and business sustainability. If you need performance and profitability improvements on a worldwide scale, perhaps we should talk.

One of my greatest strengths lies in my ability to define and implement critical strategies to heighten revenue growth, and reduce cost. For example, I led the design and implementation of self-help tools for Field Service Engineers by reducing inventory by $750,000 and shipments by 40%.

In my position as Director of Global Planning at L'Oréal, I managed the entire supply chain life cycle, providing direction of project initiatives for business process re-engineering, saving some $258,000 through establishment of early termination of service with Life Tech supply chain. I also increased product availability 3% and saved $270,000 in domestic transportation costs and $672,000 globally.

Capable of envisioning smart solutions to complex business issues, I also bring honed skills in collaborative leadership, communication, and flexibility. My past achievements show a leader with a proven track record in fast-paced and challenging environments.

Can we talk?

Sincerely,

Mike Davis

Phone (516) 843-9268
SupplychainNY@gmail.com

Tutor

To:
From:
Cc:
Subject: SAT Tutor

Dear [Name],

I am writing in reference to your opening for an English and SAT tutor. I am a dedicated student of literature and, more generally, intellectual history, and I believe I can make a real contribution to your company, for a number of reasons.

- As someone who has himself taken the SAT, ACT, and AP English and History exams in the not-so-distant past, I am familiar with not only the tests themselves but also the mental and emotional strains involved in preparing for them.

- The nature of my two areas of expertise has engendered a collateral familiarity with related disciplines, such as history, as well as a facility in acquainting myself with the rudiments of unfamiliar Humanities disciplines on short notice.

- Through my work with mentally challenged children at _____ , I have become well-versed in the patience and tact required of an educator, as well as empathetic to the challenges facing students for whom the promise of academic excellence is not compelling, or not viable.

- Because I intend to go on to graduate school and become a professor, I have a profound commitment not only to excel in teaching but to inspire in students the devotion to learning that informs every aspect of my own life. Through tutoring, I hope to learn every bit as much as students will potentially learn from me.

- Through my work as an editor and copyeditor, I have had ample experience using my knowledge of English grammar, syntax, and argument structure to improve the work of even professional authors, and doing so in a way that is both encouraging and sensitive to the feelings of the writer.

I appreciate your taking the time to review these credentials and my attached resume, and hope that we can talk soon. I am available at any time at the telephone number below.

Sincerely,

(555) 555-1234

Voice & Articulation Adjunct Faculty

To:
From:
Cc:
Subject: **Voice & Articulation** adjunct faculty

_____

Dear [Name]:

Your posting for **Voice & Articulation** adjunct faculty captured my serious interest. My 25 years' experience as a Speech Therapist in the ____ provides me with all the skills you seek.
Some key points you may find relevant include:

- ✓ _Experience assessing needs of, and providing instruction to, the disabled. In my current position, I work one-on-one with students with hearing loss, emotional disorders, ADHD, autism, and other physical disabilities impacting their ability to acquire speech. I also develop IEPs and participate in the CSE process to define students' needs and implement instruction plans._

- ✓ _Excellent leadership skills, with experience mentoring coworkers. Currently, I mentor speech therapists and teachers working with hearing-impaired students, as well as direct the activities of two other speech therapists._

- ✓ _A Master's Degree in Speech Pathology, plus NYS Certification as a Speech & Hearing Handicapped Teacher. In addition, I have attended workshops in Phonemic Awareness, Autism, and Pervasive Developmental Disorders._

In my current role, I am accountable for addressing the needs of approximately 300 elementary and secondary school students with various speech deficiencies. I believe that my knowledge and expertise would allow me to effectively serve your students in this Voice & Articulation instructional role.

Thank you for your time and consideration. I look forward to speaking with you soon. Please contact me via phone or email to arrange a mutually convenient date and time for us to meet. My resume is attached.

Sincerely,

(555) 555-1234
[_Your email address_]

Response to a Job Posting

Accounting—Job Posting

To:

From:

Cc:

Subject: Accounting CMA and GAAP opening

Dear [Name]:

I'm writing to express my interest in [name of position] posted on [where found]. As an accomplished financial professional, I have more than ten years in financial management, operational analysis, implementing effective accounting systems, and developing strategies for improving organizational performance. As a CMA, I back this up with extensive knowledge and practical application of GAAP.

Throughout my career I have maintained the highest performance standards of accounting functions. I have a proven track record of performing full-cycle accounting, including producing financial statements and supporting the financial requirements of the company for growth.

I bring excellent organizational skills, outstanding work ethic, and the ability to work in both team-oriented and self-directed environments. I would welcome the opportunity to discuss with you how I may make similar contributions to the success of your financial management team.

Thank you for your time and consideration and I do hope we can talk soon—my number is right below my signature.
Sincerely,

[Your name]
[Your telephone number]

Accounting Manager—Job Posting

To:

From:

Cc:

Subject: Ticketing Account Manager posting #4537SAM

Dear [Name],

I am applying for the position of Executive Account Manager recently posted [*ID site where job posted*]. As a former professional football player (whose career was cut short by injury) with a successful ten-year background in sales and a solid academic background, I am confident that I can make a successful contribution to your sales team. I bring a combination of strong communication and business development skills that I have leveraged to consistently exceed sales goals throughout my career. I understand the importance of cultivating customer relationships through personal contacts, and I am committed to providing a superior level of customer service to all ticket buyers. I pride myself on being dedicated to my work, self-motivated, and not afraid to take on challenges.

My skills include:

- Effective sales techniques, customer service, teamwork, and problem-solving skills.
- Ability to establish strong relationships.
- Trained in sports ticket package sales.
- Excellent communication skills and the ability to relate to customers.
- Good rapport-building skills with cold-calling techniques and sales-prospecting activities.
- Ability to handle multiple projects in a fast-paced environment.

In addition, it is my passion for sports, my previous experience in the sports industry, and my strong academic background with a BS degree in Sports and Entertainment Management and an MBA in Marketing and Strategy that sets me apart.

My resume is attached to provide more information on my strengths and career achievements. I would welcome the opportunity to discuss with you how I may make similar contributions to the success of your team. I look forward to hearing from you to schedule a personal interview.

Sincerely,

(555) 555-1234

Brand Management—Job Posting

To:

From:

Cc:

Subject: Brand Management Coordinator job posting

Dear [Name]:

Your posting on the *New York Times* website, on June 9, for a Brand Management Coordinator seems to perfectly match my background and experience. As the International Brand Coordinator for ▮▮▮▮, I coordinated meetings, prepared presentations and materials, and organized a major offsite conference. I believe that I am an excellent candidate for this position:

YOUR REQUIREMENTS	MY QUALIFICATIONS
A highly motivated, diplomatic, flexible, quality-driven professional on every project.	Successfully managed project teams involving different business units. The defined end results were achieved.
Exceptional organizational skills and attention to detail.	Planned the development and launch of the ▮▮▮▮▮▮▮▮▮▮▮▮ series. My former manager enjoyed leaving the "details" and follow-through to me.
College degree and minimum 3 years relevant business experience.	BA from Brown College. 6+ years business experience in productive, professional environments.
Computer literacy.	Extensive knowledge of Windows & Macintosh applications.

I'm interested in this position because it fits well with my new career focus in the human resources field. Currently, I am enrolled in NYU's adult career planning and development certificate program.

My resume is attached for your review. If you believe that there is a match, as I do, please call me. Thank you for your consideration.

Sincere regards,

(555) 555-1234

Clinical Pharmacist—Job Opening

To:

From:

Cc:

Subject: Clinical pharmacist opening

Dear [Name],

I was very excited to hear about your clinical pharmacist position, from our mutual colleague Amaria Ciccine, as this is a position I have been interested in for some time.

The job profile I saw on your website says you are looking for someone who works well with other health professionals and provides high-quality care and consideration to patients. I have six years' experience working with the public in a hospital setting, and consequently with an extended team of healthcare professionals.

Importantly, I have complete familiarity with the wide range of medications used in a teaching hospital and the protocols that accompany good pharmacy management in such a setting. My attached resume will show that I am dedicated to my profession, with education and experience that match your requirements for the clinical pharmacist position.

I appreciate your consideration, and I'm confident you will see a close match on evaluation of my attached resume. I look forward to talking with you. I'm just a call away.

Sincerely,

(555) 555-1234

Cloud Management—Job Posting

To:

From:

Cc:

Subject: Cloud Management

Dear [Name]:

Your job posting [insert where it was found] for a Data Center Manager fits my qualifications, and I am writing to express my interest in the position. I am the lead data center engineer at a dedicated high-security site with 1,800 enterprise servers (mainly the Samsung monsters) for a global provider of secure financial message services.

In my current position, I have maintained the hardware, software, and environment to ensure constant message flow availability at 99.999% for more than ten years; I have also maintained an incident-free six-hour CTR contract with $500K non-performance penalty.

The scope of my responsibilities includes:
- Lead storage engineer, managing schedules and workload of three rotating assistant engineers.
- Managing the integrity of a third-party site on behalf of ▮▮▮▮▮▮▮▮.
- First point of contact for resolution of all issues and face of the company for a client with globally dispersed sites.
- Increasing responsiveness while decreasing customer resolution time.
- Reducing overtime 50%.
- Running the cleanest computer storage rooms in the country.

I have been trained by one of the world's leading blue-chip technology companies to anticipate customer needs and deliver satisfaction with calm, professional consistency and technical competency. As close as anyone can in data center management, I deliver peace of mind to the client, because I anticipate and pay attention to the details.

I am accustomed to interacting at all levels of an organization and with clients throughout the technical and management hierarchies. Most notable are my strengths in facilitating cooperation among cross-functional teams and diverse corporate cultures.

I have attached my resume to provide more information on my strengths and career achievements. I would welcome the opportunity to discuss storage, cloud, and data center engineering issues with you. Can we talk?

Sincerely,

(555) 555-1234

Controller—Job Posting

To:

From:

Cc:

Subject: Controller opening

Dear [Name]:

I'm writing to express my interest in the [title] position, posted [insert where found]. I have fourteen years' financial management, operations, and investment analysis experience. As a CPA, I back this up with extensive knowledge and practical application of Generally Accepted Accounting Principles (GAAP). I'm highly analytical with a strong grasp of business imperatives, and I'm confident that I can make substantial contributions as a member of your financial management team.

Throughout my career I have maintained the highest performance standards with a diverse range of accounting and management functions. I have a proven track record of performing operational analysis and implementing effective systems and strategies to improve organizational performance. My background also includes overseeing all accounting functions for a billion-dollar insurance holding company.

I have created value in a number of ways:

- Tracking daily investment activities and calculating stock gains and losses for financial reporting to management.
- Increasing departmental revenue by 40% within three months in a new position.
- Streamlining financial and accounting operations, resulting in cost savings and increased efficiency.
- Improving collection of accounts receivable by 300% by implementing a new practice management system.
- Generating more than $40,000 net savings by resolving a sales tax audit that had remained unsettled for six years.
- Establishing accounting principles and procedures to ensure accurate and timely reporting of financial statements.

I would welcome the opportunity to discuss with you how I may make similar contributions to the success of your financial management team.

Sincerely,

(555) 555-1234

Distribution Manager—Job Posting

To:

From:

Cc:

Subject: Distribution manager 18 years' experience in aerospace

Ref: Distribution Manager posting

Dear [Name],

You are seeking an experienced and self-motivated distribution manager. I have been in distribution management with Lockheed Martin for eighteen years. I have been a distribution manager for six years.

I like to make a difference when I go to work and always look for ways to improve productivity, efficiency, and accuracy. In my current position I have identified ways to reduce downtime and waste, as well as methods to increase productivity. Performance reviews have noted my "excellent attendance and dependability" and praised me as "reliable and highly motivated."

Throughout my career, I have demonstrated my loyalty, commitment, and a solid work ethic. If you need a distribution manger who can hit the ground running, I am confident that, as a professional at the top of his professional stride, our meeting could be time well spent. My resume is attached.

Sincerely,

(555) 555-1234

Engineer—Job Posting

To:

From:

Cc:

Subject:

Dear [Name]:

I am responding to your job posting [insert where it was found] for a Quality Engineer. I believe the combination of my recent MS in Biomedical Engineering and my experience gives me an unusual set of qualifications for this job.

With a background as a research assistant and current job as a laboratory technician, I have been successful in ensuring consistency with OSHA compliance and company guidelines for quality assurance. In providing technical support, one of my strengths is to treat each customer as a key account that deserves outstanding service and response.

My skills include:
- Strong statistical, research, and data analysis skills
- Writing technical management systems reports
- Experience in quality system audits
- Troubleshooting medical equipment and securing replacement parts at the lowest cost
- Ensuring customer satisfaction by providing fast and effective solutions

I help new employees with coaching and training to help them become productive and feeling part of the team more quickly. I am committed to do everything I can to foster cooperation among cross-functional teams. I also have strong project management, presentation, and organization skills.

I would welcome the opportunity to discuss how these skills might contribute to your needs. Please find the attached copy of my resume for your review. I look forward to hearing from you to schedule a personal interview at your convenience.

Sincerely,

(555) 555-1234

Engineering Management—Job Posting

To:

From:

Cc:

Subject: Engineering Management, 20 patents

Dear [Name]:

I have wide experience in production processes and Six Sigma and have been awarded over twenty patents. I rarely make career moves, but I am looking for a new home with a great engineering team. With fifteen-plus years in engineering management, my strengths lie in design process, innovation, business strategies, and process improvements.

My professional goals have always been to drive initiatives for innovation and process improvements to consistently meet strategic goals. My track record clearly demonstrates abilities as an engineering manager and a decision-maker with a clear vision and focus on efficiency, productivity, and innovations for systems improvement.

As an engineering manager, I create value in a number of ways including:

- Responding to customer needs with innovative design solutions and enhancements.
- Developing patentable technologies yielding profitable solutions and IP ownership delivering technical and strategic advantages for the company.
- Implementing product and process improvements for cost optimization and DFM, consistently meeting or exceeding annual savings targets.
- Developing, training, and mentoring engineers on the innovations and invention processes, developing new generations of technical innovators.

With my extensive experience and knowledge of engineering and operations, I believe I would make a valuable contribution to your team and help lead the company to further success. I have attached my resume to provide more information. Can we talk?

Sincerely,

[Your name]
[Your telephone number]

Marketing and Communications—Job Posting

To:
From:
Cc:

Subject: Communications & Marketing Professional Position

Dear [Name],

Your Communications & Marketing opportunity posted in [where you found the posting] is tailored to my ability to plan, develop, and execute strategies that facilitate communication between the organization, the media, and the general public.

I have in-depth experience developing and executing well-defined communication strategies that increase brand awareness and generate traffic and readership. My track record confirms my ability to generate a strong organic following in support of both internal and external communication initiatives.

I thrive on the demands of finding solutions to complex problems and I am confident that I can help [company name] meet the challenges outlined in your recent posting. The attached resume, although detailed and comprehensive, does not fully demonstrate the dedication, drive, and integrity I bring to my work. Thank you for your time and consideration. I look forward to hearing from you and hope we can talk soon.

Sincerely,

(555) 555-1234

Organizational Development Analyst—Job Posting

To:

From:

Cc:

Subject: Organizational Development Analyst

Dear [Name]:

I am writing to express my interest in your Organizational Development Analyst position [insert where found]. With five years of organizational development experience, I work to develop effective learning and performance programs that meet the company's organizational goals.

I have worked with a Fortune 1000 company and a start-up in the consumer goods industry in development and design of training and OD programs. My areas of focus include learning and development programs, organizational development programs, and performance management.

As a learning and organizational development manager, I add value in a number of ways:

- Conduct needs assessments and identify performance gaps.
- Plan, design, and implement Organizational Development (OD) training programs.
- Provide continuous improvements to existing training programs.
- Develop measurement and evaluation tools to evaluate program efficiency and effectiveness.

I have experience interacting at all levels of an organization and with clients. I have attached my resume to provide more information on my work history and capabilities. I would welcome the opportunity to discuss learning and OD programs. I hope we can talk soon.

Sincerely,

[Your name]
[Your telephone number]

Product Marketing Management—Job Posting

To:

From:

Cc:

Subject: Product Marketing Management position / AMAQRT45

Dear [Name]:

I am a multilingual and multicultural marketing professional with product and project management experience. I'm a team player and leader by example, experienced with metrics and vendor contract negotiations.

I am dedicated to quality results and the execution of successful campaigns for both the company and the client. Plus, I have the analytical experience to align customer needs with business requirements and the ability to nurture strategic partnerships that support consistent growth. Specifically I have:

- Operated as a focal pivot between manufacturing, marketing, sales, and customers, resulting in improved response time, margins, order rates, and customer satisfaction.
- Improved product-pricing system for technology products, reducing quote response time 134%, delivering $2.3 M higher annual margins.
- Planned and managed logistics of inventory management, margin enhancement, and profit benchmarks to help the company reach its objectives.
- Developed pricing strategies, monitored market trends, and recommended course corrections as necessary.
- Analyzed P&L statements to ensure profit objectives and revenue targets were being met.
- Priced product line globally and tracked trade and intercompany business using my database management expertise.
- Coordinated and maintained all requests for competitive crossing information globally.

I would welcome the opportunity to discuss how I can make similar contributions to your team. Thanks for your time and consideration, and I do hope we can talk soon.
Sincerely,

[Your name]
[Your telephone number]

Senior Accountant—Job Posting

To:

From:

Cc:

Subject: Senior accountant – (posting S.A Fin.56)

Dear [Name]:

I am writing to express my interest in the Senior Accountant position, posted on your website.

With ten-plus years' experience with general accounting, administrative experience, and strong analytical skills, I have always maintained the highest performance standards across a diverse range of accounting functions:

- Manage general ledger, bank statements, A/P, A/R, P&L, balance sheets, budgets and forecasting, financial statements, and payroll.
- Create financial analysis reports for management and bid statements for sales and marketing.
- Implement and enforce accounting standards to ensure integrity and accuracy.
- Assist management in identifying, designing, and implementing more efficient work processes.
- Assist in miscellaneous administrative duties such as payroll and general HR tasks.

I take pride in coupling accounting knowledge and business judgment to help facilitate efficient and accurate workflow. I communicate effectively with all levels of the organization and with vendors, and I bring a genuine love and respect for my work, delivering high productivity in both team-oriented and self-directed environments.
If you have need for an accountant to quickly become a productive and loyal member of your accounting team, I would welcome the opportunity to talk with you. My resume is attached and my telephone number is below my signature.

Sincerely,

(555) 555-1234

Tech Public Relations—Job Posting

To:

From:

Cc:

Subject: Technology PR

Dear [Name],

As a high-tech PR professional with fifteen years' technology experience, I possess the proven skills and drive that you are known for. My specific experience includes:

Point of Strategic Counsel
Primary contact for creation, execution, and delivery of messaging and launch strategies for both companies and C-level executives. This has resulted in repeat business as loyal clients stay with me over the years.

Manage High-Level Influential Relations with Key Press
I constantly develop and nurture relationships with key media, and understand the importance of managing those relationships with integrity, respect, reliability, and discretion. This has enabled me to craft and place stories in all major TV, radio, print, and digital media outlets.

Coach Team and Account Staff
I learned over the years that a team is only as good as its leader and it's more rewarding to be on the winning team. I lead by example, believe in positive reinforcement and recognition, and keep team members focused on our clients' objectives.

The attached resume will give you further insight into my capabilities. I feel confident that a meeting would demonstrate that my high-tech public relations expertise would be a worthy addition to your team. I look forward to speaking with you soon.

Regards,

(555) 555-1234

DIRECT APPROACH TO A COMPANY

Career Change—Marketing to Finance

To:
From:
Cc:
Subject: Finance: Accounting Manager/Director, Controller/Treasurer
_____

Dear [Name],

I have ten years' successful experience within financial services marketing, and will receive my CPA within two months. With this unique combination of skills and awareness, I now hope to segue into a more distinct financial management position such as accounting Manager, Controller, or Treasurer.

As an Account Manager in financial services, I know many different industries, and my marketing savvy would be of unusual benefit to any company seeking someone with these titles.

My understanding of the revenue generating function *and* the revenue protection and leveraging function, especially of financial services companies, gives me a very special frame of reference on my chosen path. As an executive recruiter, I am sure you can appreciate this.

I have attached my resume, which will flesh out my unusual and desirable background; I would appreciate your input. I am available for interviews, and can be reached at (555) 555-1234. Please consider me available as a resource for your other searches within my profession.

Yours truly,

(555) 555-1234

Career Change to Teaching

To:
From:
Cc:
Subject: Japanese-Speaking English Teacher

Dear [Name],

With this letter, I would like to introduce myself and share my sincere motivation to teach English in Japan. My experience as a substitute middle school teacher has helped me to understand methods of student interaction and reach a level of comfort in the classroom.

I strive to build relationships with students and to facilitate classroom activities and inspire the learners. It is something I truly enjoy.

The _____ website encourages "all outgoing, dynamic, and flexible people to apply." In my current position as a flight attendant for Hawaii Wings Airlines, I am required to demonstrate these characteristics daily. Communication and quick-thinking skills are a must onboard an aircraft full of passengers. Flexibility is essential in the areas of customer service, in interaction with colleagues, and in work scheduling.

My motivation is indeed genuine. I speak conversational Japanese and I look forward to the possibility of discussing the opportunity with you. I will gladly make myself available for a telephone or videoconference interview. My resume is attached for your review.

Respectfully,

(555) 555-1234

Career Change to Railroad Industry

To:
From:
Cc:
Subject: 20 years in transportation

Dear [Name],

With 20 years' experience in transportation, I am seeking a job opportunity that will help me achieve my long-time goal of working in the railroad industry.

Attached for your review is a resume that briefly outlines my relevant qualifications. Some of the key skills that I believe make me a strong candidate for a position with your rail line include:

- **Significant experience as an Equipment Operator and Truck Driver.**

- **Experience dispatching for the New York State Dept. of Transportation.**

- **An excellent aptitude and desire to learn new tasks.**

- **An enjoyment of and willingness to work outdoors—in all weather conditions.**

- **Exceptional attention to detail and accuracy in my work.**

- **Responsible worker who is dedicated to consistently exceeding expectations.**

I understand the structure of the rail industry and am more than willing to accept an entry-level position (and all the challenges that go with it) in order to get the opportunity to break in with a railroad line. I would enjoy speaking with you in person about how I could fill a need for your company. I look forward to talking with you soon; please email or call me at (555) 555-1234.

Sincerely,

(555) 555-1234

Chief Financial Officer

To:
From:
Cc:
Subject: CFO, global and boardroom performer

Dear [Name],

As a Chief Financial Officer, I have built a reputation for strategic business and financial planning for global corporations. My ability to identify challenges to, and capitalize upon, opportunities to expand revenue growth, reduce operating costs, and improve overall productivity has always been one of my strongest assets.

My strengths in financial and accounting management as well as my thorough understanding of finance operations have vastly contributed to my career and success as a leader. I maintain the self-confidence, credibility, and stature to make things happen with colleagues. Just as significant are my abilities to develop rapport among subordinates, coworkers, executive management groups, and the board.

My objective is to secure a position as a CFO or Vice President, and to pursue new opportunities with an organization providing new and exciting challenges. Having a complete picture of my expertise and experience is very important. As you will note in my resume, I have made significant contributions to my employers, and take my job very seriously.

I appreciate your time and consideration, and will be in contact next week to see if we are able to schedule a meeting date for an interview. I look forward to speaking with you soon. My resume is attached for your review.

Regards,

(555) 555-1234

Compliance Project Analyst—Direct Approach

To:

From:

Cc:

Subject: Compliance Project Analyst

Dear [Name],

I'd like to be your next Compliance Project Analyst. My qualifications include:

- Five years of financial services experience, most recently as a Mortgage Change Agent for ▮▮ Bank.
- Strengths in project management, technical writing, and mortgage escrow records management.
- In-depth knowledge of U.S. banking and mortgage lending regulations.
- Mortgage Servicing Certification and Lean Six Sigma–Green Belt Certification.

In brief, I am a business process analyst and effective change agent who thrives on steep challenges. I am focused and analytical with the energy for sustained action, the ability to build consensus in support of change initiatives for regulatory compliance, and the tenacity to deliver. I can define the scope, monitor the progress, and create communications to ensure effective implementation and measure adoption.

I am confident that I have the leadership qualities, regulatory compliance knowledge, and technical writing skills you are seeking. My resume is attached for your evaluation.

Sincerely,

(555) 555-1234

Credit-Collections

To:
From:
Cc:
Subject: Credit/Collections applications job posting
_____

Dear [Name],

I bring 18+ years of accounts receivable experience in addition to being involved in all processing stages of collections, resolving payment issues, and collecting on past due payments. The scope of my experience includes, but is not limited to, commercial, automotive, and manufacturing environments.

I focus on delivering results and providing superior service by quickly identifying problem areas in accounts receivable and developing a solution strategy to ensure issues are resolved. My expertise lies in my strong ability to build rapport with clients, analyze accounts, and manage all aspects related to my appointed position and areas of responsibilities.

Due to circumstances beyond my control, I was unable to continue my employment as a cash applications analyst with a well-known automotive industry leader. My objective is to secure a position in accounts receivable and credit collections with an established company.

My attached resume details my skills, experience, and the contributions I have made to employers. I look forward to speaking with you soon and answering any questions you may have regarding my background, and I will follow up with you next week.

Regards,

(555) 555-1234

Direction Shift Within Sales

To:
From:
Cc:
Subject: B-to-B sales professional

Dear [Name],

Having spent five years as an executive recruiter, I realize how many resumes you receive on a daily basis. I also remember how valuable a few always turned out to be.

My background, skills, and talents are in all aspects of sales and sales management. As job search is the only field of sales where the products talk back, I am confident that my skills will readily translate into less complex sales environments. My research indicates that your expertise is in this broad Sales/ Marketing area.

I have attached my resume, which highlights my skills and supports my objectives. I would appreciate the opportunity to meet and exchange ideas. I will call you over the next few days to make an appointment. If you prefer, you may reach me by email or in the evening at (555) 555-1234.

Thank you; I look forward to speaking with you.

Sincerely,

(555) 555-1234

Director of Health Services—Direct Approach

To:
From:
Cc:
Subject: Director Health Services

Dear [Name],

If you are interested in dramatically improving the performance and profitability of your organization, I am a performance-focused director of health services with two decades of experience that comprises a history of leading innovative projects to drive improvements in overall healthcare access, quality of care, affordability, and profitability.

In my current position as Director for Supervisory Health Services for ███████ ███████████, I led the design and implemented two Affordable Care Act–mandated projects. Additional accomplishments include:

- Drove improvements in communication between CMS components throughout the United States, contributing to overall identification and resolution of Part D implementation issues.
- Accelerated growth in beneficiary enrollments in four PDPs, earning the following awards: On-the-Spot Cash Award, Administrator's Achievement Award (2), and Special Achievement Award (2).
- Communicated with CMS partners in eight CMS regions across the country, providing strategic quality assessment of two Medicare/Medicaid programs.
- Established a $1.6 million contract with oversight of home health services, serving as Government Task Lead to improve quality of care.

Capable of envisioning smart solutions to complex business issues, I am now ready to move to a new challenge in an arena where my unique skills and knowledge can deliver immediate value and long-term solutions. I look forward to hearing from you (my phone number is immediately below my signature) and learning more about your plans, needs, and goals and how I might contribute to achieving them.

Sincerely,

[Your name]
[Your telephone number]

Entry Level—Direct Approach

To:

From:

Cc:

Subject: Entry-level museum management

Dear [Name]:

I am a qualified exhibit interpreter and volunteer at museums with more than four years' volunteer experience in roles involving extensive contact with the public. My passion is to develop my career in the museum profession with a focus on supporting education in the museum setting.

I have a solid academic education with a BA in Philosophy with a minor in Communications and I am committed to ongoing professional development classes that further my knowledge and qualifications for exhibit interpretation; I regularly monitor museum tours on my time off to develop my presentation and teaching skills in a museum environment.

I feel that I can add value in the following ways:

- My communication skills motivate and educate visitors by interpreting exhibits and by using interactive materials to enhance the learning experience.
- My interpersonal skills enable me to work with visitors of all ages and cultures.
- My passion fuels my knowledge on museum exhibitions, collections, programs, tours, and events.
- My attitude ensures a welcoming atmosphere and engages visitors and encourages their involvement in museum activities—increasing our relevance to the community.
- I am always involved in community outreach programs.

I am reliable, dependable, and take great pride and pleasure in my work. My resume is attached, and I would welcome the opportunity to discuss any role that can use these skills. Thank you for your consideration, and I look forward to hearing from you.

Sincerely,

(555) 555-1234

Entry-Level Media Production

To:

From:

Cc:

Subject: Entry-Level Media Production
_____

Dear [Name],

Do you need a tenacious and driven Production Assistant? Having completed classes, I will be granted a BA in Journalism from _____ in December, but I am eager to start my career now. I held two jobs while attending school, and will have completed my degree in three years. It is with the same passion, integrity, and energy that I intend to pursue my career.

_"I would rank Ms. _____'s work in the top 10% of students I have taught; she is not afraid to tackle tough projects; I believe she has the ability to quickly make positive contributions."_
**** *******, Ph.D., Chairperson, Department of Communications, _____ College

"_____ was an exemplary Journalism major. She took charge of the tasks given to her and performed them in a superior manner. I admire her strong enthusiasm and her attention to detail."
****** ****, Assistant Director of Television Technical Operations, _____ College

I possess the talent for a career in media and an understanding of how demanding it can be. But unlike most, I am willing to "pay the price" of hard work, rough work schedules, and the total availability that the industry requires.

I am eager to learn more about the challenges facing your organization and to discuss how I can make a difference. Please review my attached resume, and thanks so much for your consideration.

Regards,

(555) 555-1234

Entry-Level Pharmaceutical Sales

To:

From:

Cc:

Subject: Entry-Level Pharmaceutical Sales

Dear [Name],

Since you are one of the most respected pharmaceutical companies in the industry, I am eager to make a contribution to your team as a Pharmaceutical Sales Representative.

As a recent graduate with a BA in Marketing, my professional experience is limited. However, I believe you will find that I exhibit intelligence, common sense, initiative, maturity, and stability. I would also like to bring these three relevant points to your attention:

1. As the daughter of a physician, sister of a nurse, and cousin of a surgeon, I have had a lifetime of exposure to the medical community, and this gives me a greater than expected grounding in healthcare and its terminology compared to most candidates.
2. It also gives me insight into the way physicians think, evaluate, and make decisions. For example, I know product presentations must be made in a timely, succinct, and caring manner for successful sales in this industry.
3. In the last 18 months, since I made my decision to join the pharmaceutical industry, I have had intensive tutoring from family members.

I believe you will be impressed with my grasp of the sales process, and very pleasantly surprised with the depth of my understanding of the people who make up the target customer base.

After reviewing the attached resume, please email or contact me at (555) 555-1234 to arrange an interview. I look forward to discussing how my qualifications can meet your personnel needs and contribute to your company's important mission.

Sincerely,

(555) 555-1234

Environmental Health and Safety Director—Direct Approach

To:

From:

Cc:

Subject: Control EH&S costs

Dear [Name]:

I am a seasoned EH&S director with extensive knowledge and hands-on experience in the oil and gas industry. I am knowledgeable in OSHA, EPA, and DOT policies and regulations, coupled with a sound academic education and extensive background in the United States Army. As a multifaceted, diversely trained safety professional, I see the EH&S as a cost containment center, while additionally contributing to community relations and company PR.

I have saved companies significant amounts of money by creating programs to ensure up-to-date training and regulatory compliance that minimize workplace accidents and environmental litigation. I believe that accidents are preventable and a root cause determination is paramount to prevent recurrence and an integral part of the work.

As an EH&S director I have created value in a number of ways including:
- Initiating contractor management programs for vendors with poor safety records to assist in improving safety training and practices.
- Establishing an Air Quality Department to write air permits, collect emissions data, and prepare state and federally required reports.
- Initiating systems for investigating potential real estate purchases for environmental and safety issues.

I have a proven record of raising the level of safety for employees, reducing injuries, and assisting companies dedicated to lowering risks while increasing company profitability. I take pride in creating a culture of safety, including executive presence helpful in advising management on EH&S analysis and procedures. I bring an outstanding work ethic and the ability to demonstrate the financial benefits to smart EH&S policies.

I would welcome the opportunity to discuss with you how I may make similar contributions to the success of your EH&S team. My resume and phone number are below my signature. I look forward to hearing from you.

Sincerely,

[Your name]
[Your telephone number]

Financial Reporting Project Management—Direct Approach

To:

From:

Cc:

Subject: Financial Reporting Project Management

Dear [Name]:

I am a senior project manager with experience in financial reporting and analysis, large-scale project management, and staff supervision My ability to establish rapport with executives and cross-functional leaders speeds delivery of financial reports for data-driven analytical decision-making and keeps projects on schedule and within budget.

I am skilled in creating project dashboards, giving C-level presentations, and facilitating meetings. I have experience training, developing, and evaluating employees, as well as coordinating cross-functional and virtual teams. I am a proactive problem solver with the ability to communicate and break down complex data in a clear and concise manner.
I also bring strong technical and instructional writing experience, including RFP analysis and scoring, inventory burn-down plans, and working knowledge of facility and infrastructure support, including IT systems/software integration.

My project management experience includes requirements definition, business case development, project controls, change management, risk assessment, resource allocation, vendor/subcontractor relationship management, inventory management, logistics, purchasing, invoicing, licensing, insurance coverage, hardware/software installation, team management, conflict resolution, design/implementation of business system improvements, and international facility build experience.

Details of the above are attached in my resume. I would welcome the opportunity to discuss how my experience developing action plans, scheduling, project planning, and supervising professional and technical staff could be of service to your organization. Can we set up a meeting?

Sincerely,

(555) 555-1234

General Counsel—Direct Approach

To:

From:

Cc:

Subject: Latin America–experienced General Counsel

Dear [Name]:

After ten years as managing partner for a top Brazilian law firm, I am seeking a position as General Counsel for an American corporation with financial interests in Latin America. I bring a deep understanding of Latin American trade as well as fluency in English and Portuguese along with working business Spanish.

My qualifications include:

- Ability to provide sound legal advice to corporate management in support of global commercial operations and growth.
- Specialty in large-scale e-commerce, tax, energy, and infrastructure projects.
- Experience in overseas investments, mergers and acquisitions, joint ventures, and reorganizations.
- Skill in contract negotiation and administration, dispute resolution, arbitration, and litigation.
- Strengths in strategic planning that include the ability to analyze financial data, frame issues, and provide targeted, actionable advice to achieve the success of critical missions.

My resume is attached and I am eager to repeat and surpass my prior achievements with a U.S.–based organization. May I have an appointment for a personal interview to discuss the possibilities? My telephone number is below my signature.

Sincerely,

(555) 555-1234

Healthcare Systems Management—Direct Approach

To:

From:

Cc:

Subject: Healthcare Systems Management

___

Dear [Name],

Leading technology initiatives to drive systems performance, cut operational costs, and increase profitability is what I do best.

I bring fifteen years' experience delivering advanced technology solutions for regional hospitals and healthcare facilities and leading teams of highly skilled IT professionals in massive technology conversions and integrations projects. For the past seven years I have worked as Director of Technology for ███████████████████████, where I provided strategic IT direction to bridge the gap between technology and business priorities.

Over the years, I've learned that any project is only as successful as the IT team that implements and supports the technology. Aside from continued professional development, success stems from respectful communications, empowering employees to perform at their personal best each day, and teamwork. My qualifications include an MBA and BS in Management Information Systems, plus Lean Six Sigma and Change Management Certifications.

Let's schedule a time to meet to discuss how my leadership, technical, and managerial skills might best serve your company. My resume and phone number are below my signature. Can we talk?

Sincerely,

[Your name]
[Your telephone number]

Inside Sales

To:

From:

Cc:

Subject: Telephone Sales

Dear [Name],

My first job in sales management was right out of college, running a beach bar. My competitors were like pesky flies—they kept popping up everywhere, opening with lots of glitz, taking all the customers, and then crashing and burning after six months. But during those six months they were trying to take all <u>my</u> customers!

These were serious challenges, to which I responded with the best strategies and tactics I could coordinate—free pool playing, fruity drinks for girls, sports TV for the guys. I even gave away free beer one night.

Today I am the same aggressive, ambitious sales professional I was then. OK . . . these days I wouldn't give away free beer, but I <u>do</u> respond to sales challenges with all the competitiveness, creativity, and customer concern in my heart. In my last sales position, I was quite successful selling vacation packages by telephone for several reasons:

- I qualified my targets well.
- I was knowledgeable about the product and customers' motivators for that product.
- I think well and profitably on my feet.
- I'm honest and a natural rapport builder.

The point of my attached resume is that I would like to talk with you about putting my sales, problem-solving, and customer service skills to work for your organization. When can we meet? My resume is attached for your review.

Sincerely,

Your Name

Internal Promotion—Direct Approach

To:

From:

Cc:

Subject: RE: Campus Library Director PIN 1826

_____

Dear [Name],

I am responding to your job posting for a Campus Library Director. I have had the pleasure of working with these students across the Information Services Desk at the library for a number of years. Becoming your Library Director is the right place for me to land after my more than fifteen years of professional experience with increasing levels of responsibility at the University. I would greatly enjoy the opportunity to ensure our students receive outstanding library services in every place they gather—online, and on or off campus.

I believe I am an excellent candidate for this position as I have illustrated below:

Your Requirements	My Qualifications
• Ten years of progressively responsible professional/technical experience in area assigned	• 15 years of library experience with increasing responsibility in innovative, customer-focused environment.
• Leadership and supervisory experience	• 7 years of successful staff management in a high-traffic research library environment. Proven ability to inspire a shared vision.
• Master's Degree in Library/Information Science from an ALA-accredited university	• MLS and continued professional education in leadership and technology.

On top of this I already know this library, the staff, customers and vendors. I would welcome the opportunity to meet with your selection team to discuss the results you would expect from the new Library Director. Thank you for your time and consideration. I look forward to an email or phone call from you soon. My resume is attached for your consideration.

Sincerely,

(555) 555-1234
Attachment: resume

International Relations Intern

To:

From:

Cc:

Subject: International Relations Intern

Dear [Name],

I am interested in being considered for an internship. I am currently a senior at the University of _____ majoring in International Studies with a concentration in Latin America and a minor in Political Science. I speak and write Spanish.

Previous internships have increased my knowledge of International Relations and have enabled me to make use of my education in a professional environment. I am very serious about my education and future career, and am eager to learn as much as possible throughout my internship.

My references will confirm that I tackle any task, no matter how humble or complex, with skill and enthusiasm. As a highly motivated professional, I enjoy the challenge of complex, demanding assignments. My well-developed writing and communication skills are assets when dealing with such challenges.

I would welcome the opportunity to discuss how I could make a contribution to your organization as an intern. Please review my attached resume; I look forward to talking with you soon. Thank you.

Sincerely,

(555) 555-1234

IT Strategic Systems—Direct Approach

To:

From:

Cc:

Subject: IT Strategic Systems solution

Dear [Name],

Leading technology projects, teams, and organizations to support strategic business goals is my wheelhouse. I back up this statement with an MBA in International Business and twelve years of IT project management experience. Currently I am the Director of IT Strategic Systems Development for a company with $45 million in annual revenue. Here are two IT transformation initiatives that capture my capabilities:

- Cutting spending by 70% and significantly decreased IT staff hours used to maintain server hardware by collaborating with Amazon Web Services to forge a cloud migration plan that is PCI compliant.
- Increasing revenues by 30% through the design/implementation of a customized program for ████ on speculation, resulting in the company winning the ████ account and increasing company revenues by 30%.

Of course, technology services are only as good as the technical staff that designs, implements, and supports them. My superiors have recognized me for building cohesive, high-performing teams. I have successfully managed geographically dispersed teams of engineers, administrators, and analysts (including contractors, outsource partners, and offshore resources) through all phases of technology integration and transformation projects.

Currently I am exploring executive-level technology management positions where I can enhance the operational and financial success of a company by introducing new technologies, upgrading existing resources, bringing cutting-edge products and services to market, and developing a strong and sustainable competitive lead.

Can we talk? My number is beneath my signature.

Sincerely,

(555) 555-1234

Litigation Attorney—Direct Approach

To:

From:

Cc:

Subject: Litigation attorney

Dear [Name]:

Are you looking for a commercial litigation attorney with outstanding communications and client-management skills? I am a highly motivated litigator with the tenacity and analytical skills you would expect. I am actively seeking a position with broader responsibilities where I can put my experience to work.

I offer:

- Dual licensure in New York and New Jersey.
- Strong business acumen and ten years of legal experience.
  - Five years as a paralegal and law clerk and five years as an attorney.
  - Specializing in products liability, toxic tort, class action, fraud, and unfair business practices.
- Oral advocacy, negotiation, mediation, and litigation skills.
- Research, documentation, and legal review skills.
- Exceptional customer relationship management skills.

I admire your law firm and would welcome an interview; my resume is attached, and I hope that after reading you will give me a call.

Sincerely,

(555) 555-1234

Managed Care Coordinator—Direct Approach

To:

From:

Cc:

Subject: Managed Care Coordinator

Dear [Name],

As a recent graduate with a Master's in Health Administration, I am seeking a position as a Managed Care Coordinator. I bring three years of knowledge and experience in the healthcare industry, along with a strong desire to drive improvements to healthcare access and quality of care.

In my current position as a Customer Service Representative for ██████████████ I provide support to ███████ members and ██████ Medicaid members by assisting with benefits, billing, and payments.

In addition to my outstanding customer service skills, I have served as an intern for ████████████████ School of Medicine where I developed knowledge and experience of managed healthcare, requiring me to conduct research on top-selling medical oncology drugs, which improved drug reimbursements.

Additional accomplishments include:

- Surpassed all quality objectives by achieving 93% customer service score.
- Gained extensive knowledge of Medicare and Medicaid rules and regulations.

I am now ready to move on to a new challenge where my skills and knowledge can bring immediate value and long-term benefits. My resume and phone number are beneath my signature. I look forward to hearing from you in the near future to schedule an interview.

Sincerely,

[Your name]
[Your telephone number]

Merchandising—Direct Approach

To:

From:

Cc:

Subject: Merchandising position

Dear [Name],

I am writing to express my interest in the Assistant Merchant position posted on your website. I have a combined background of three years' retail merchandising experience, plus a BS in Fashion Technology.

I have worked in organizational support and financial research and analysis for the merchandising team, and I'm experienced in sales events and product placement. Specifically I have:

- Worked with cross-functional teams and understand what it takes to coordinate interdepartmental activities in support of merchandising goals.
- Produced weekly and monthly sales reports.
- In coordination with buyer, assisted with merchandise selection and buying for the largest retail sales event of the year, resulting in 110% of target sales.
- Conducted in-store visits to ensure the implementation and execution of seasonal plans.
- Revamped stationery category and introduced new products to fit customer purchasing trends, resulting in increased sales in stationery category.
- Launched new service enhancements providing opportunities for cross-selling and leveraging existing infrastructure, resulting in 200% revenue increase.
- Coordinated plans and launch of new products, working with sales and operations executives.

These skills and my experience seem to match your needs well and I would welcome the opportunity to discuss how I could become a productive member of your team. Thanks for your time and consideration and I do hope we can talk soon.

Sincerely,

[Your name]
[Your telephone number]

Merchandising—Entry Level

To:

From:

Cc:

Subject: Retail Merchandizing

Dear [Name]:

I have had a passion for the fashion all my life and I moved to New York to make this happen. I am enthusiastically applying for the [name] Internship recently posted [where you found the posting].

I am a multilingual and multicultural professional with experience in the design-manufacturing-to-market cycle from a prior internship. I also bring experience in boutique design and interior decoration, plus a good grounding in fabric and their applications from family business and upbringing.

As a professional I always strive to create value, and in my experience to date have:

- Arranged advertising, marketing content, and strategically placed advertisements to attract desired target market.
- Scheduled client appointments, managed records, negotiated with vendors, and provided customer service excellence.

I have a very strong interest in pursuing a career in the fashion industry and believe I possess the ability and initiative to consistently deliver on my responsibilities as an intern. I would be delighted to have the opportunity for a personal interview. Thank you in advance for your time and consideration.

Sincerely,

Sincerely,

(555) 555-1234

Military to Civilian

Dear [Name],

In anticipation of completing my military service in April 2011, I am seeking a civilian position that will capitalize on my experience and training as a US Navy Registered Nurse. I believe that my clinical background and specialized training in emergency response and crisis management would make me an asset to your nursing staff. With this in mind, I have attached a resume for your review that outlines my credentials.

Some key points you may find relevant include:

- **Caring for a broad array of patients, ranging from infants to senior citizens, and including post-operative, medical, infectious disease, oncology, and end-of-life scenarios.**

- **Developing rapport with diverse cultural groups, both in clinical and social settings. The patients I have dealt with cut across the full spectrum of ethnic and socioeconomic strata, from enlisted personnel to flag officers and their dependents.**

- **Completing training and engaging in field exercises that have prepared me for disaster response in a civilian community.**

I am confident that my dedication to caring for patients, and desire to become an integral part of a treatment team, would allow me to make a significant contribution to the health and well-being of your patients.

Please contact me via phone or email to discuss how I might fulfill your needs in a clinical nursing role. Thank you for your time and consideration. I look forward to speaking with you soon.

Sincerely,

(555) 555-1234

Military to Civilian Transition

To:
From:
Cc:
Subject: Sys admin/people skills/military background

Dear [Name],

If you seek a new Systems Administrator who is technically proficient and has verifiable interpersonal skills, then we have good reason to talk. Whatever the Sys Admin challenge, I've done it, done it under fire, and can handle whatever you throw at me; that's my military training speaking.

I possess extensive technical skills and experience. My primary focus has been on Windows NT. In fact, I am currently pursuing my Microsoft Certified Systems Engineer designation. My plans are to attain this at about the time I leave the military in two months, when I will be able to bring this added expertise to an employer. My attached resume has all the details.

More difficult to portray on a resume are people skills. My job is to serve as a support person, there to keep the system operating smoothly for end-users, as well as to provide them training. Colleagues, supervisors, subordinates, and end-users will confirm my interpersonal skills during reference checks.

Sys Admin is a team and cross-functional team effort. I have commendations for my abilities as a team player as well as a team leader and a verifiable track record in taking projects and running with them, but the successes are a result of the combined efforts of the whole team.

A meeting at your convenience would be greatly appreciated. I look forward to speaking with you in the near future. Please review my attached resume.

Sincerely,

(555) 555-1234

Pharmaceutical Sales Management—Direct Approach

To:

From:

Cc:

Subject: Pharma Sales Management

I am an accomplished sales professional with more than eighteen years of pharmaceutical sales experience, including ten years in the National Account Segment. I have exceptional skills in all stages of the sales cycle backed by numerous awards and progressive promotions for exceeding sales quotas and company objectives. As an experienced national account director working with talented sales teams, I've won national performance management awards for the last eight years.

In my current position as Director, National Accounts ▮▮▮▮▮▮, I develop contracting strategies that support the launch of new products and build relationships with decision-makers at Medicare intermediaries (MACs), commercial payers, Group Purchasing Organizations (GPOs), and key opinion leaders in the oncology marketplace. I also collaborate with scientific and marketing team members to create strategically designed customer-oriented messaging.

I have been progressively promoted to my current responsibilities due to my problem-solving skills, persistence, teamwork, and resourcefulness applied to closing sales and keeping clients. I naturally offer superior negotiating and presentation skills. In addition, I am skilled in identifying new business opportunities and closing deals, two qualities that have helped make significant contributions to my employer's growth.

I have attached my resume to provide more information on my background. With my extensive experience and knowledge of the healthcare market, I believe I would make a valuable contribution to your team. I would very much like to schedule a personal meeting where we can further discuss my qualifications. May we meet to discuss your needs further?

Sincerely,

[Your name]
[Your telephone number]

Procurement—Direct Approach

To:

From:

Cc:

Subject: Procurement challenges

Dear [Name],

As a skilled leader with more than twenty years in manufacturing and procurement, I know that growing organizations require leaders to wear many hats. I am a hands-on leader and accustomed to modeling success for my staff. This insight affords me quick acceptance into the culture of any organization and relevance at all levels. A bottom-up view also reveals opportunity areas for quick improvement that evade the traditional top-down leader. Highlights of my capabilities include:

Throughout my career, I have consistently turned around underperforming operations into high-growth profit centers. During my time with ██████, I increased productivity 25%, annual volume production 500%, and drove improvements of key quality indicators 23%. These accomplishments are just a small sample of the success I will bring to your organization.

Additional accomplishments and highlights include:

- Led the design and implementation of corporate procedures related to Central Global Procurement.
- Performed negotiation of $150 million in contracts, exceeding budget expectations for eight consecutive years.
- Delivered $44 million in savings by creating new sourcing strategies and managing supply base of 530 international suppliers.
- Led turnaround of the Romania facility within three months, realizing an increase of throughput 111%, productivity 27%, and quality KPIs 25%.

I encourage you to read further about my achievements in the attached resume. I look forward to discussing your company's future goals and how I can assist. Please feel free to contact me at the phone number or email address as detailed above.

Sincerely,

(555) 555-1234

Production Assistant, Publishing

To:

From:

Cc:

Subject: PA Publishing
_____

Dear [Name]:

In the interest of exploring opportunities in the publishing industry, I have enclosed my resume for your review. Over the last two years, I have gained valuable knowledge and experience in many aspects of personnel assistance, office procedures, and administrative operations.

Recently I volunteered my time to edit a cookbook, and have been responsible for editing the newsletter for my sorority. I consider myself a good writer and an avid reader, and have always wanted to get into publishing.

With my considerable energy, drive, and ability to work long hours, I believe I could make a positive contribution to your organization, and I would appreciate the opportunity to discuss my qualifications at your earliest convenience.

Thank you for your time and consideration. I look forward to meeting with you. My resume is attached for your review.

Respectfully,

(555) 555-1234

King Lee

San Francisco   (415) 983-5349   [username]@GMail.com

[Month, Day], 2017

[Name]
[Address]
[City, State Zip]

Dear [Name],

Spearheading major software development initiatives for the manufacturing industry defines my project management and leadership skills. I am experienced managing the entire software development life cycle, from initial design to delivery and support. My skills include systems documentation, software application testing, technology implementations, and training to deliver large-scale projects on time, while meeting all customer requirements.

Most recently at ███████████ I assisted in the design, development, deployment, and sale of a $980,000 ████ application package. I also instituted offshore initiatives to reduce cost while streamlining processes. Additional accomplishments include:

- Realized $125,000 savings with an inventory auditing system to meet external auditor requirements and led a full physical inventory for $23 million in parts to ensure integrity and usability.
- Reduced costs up to $60 million a year in potential penalties by ensuring compliance with U.S. government export regulations.

For organizations requiring professionals with proven project management, leadership, and superior interpersonal skills, my unique skill set and experiences can play a key role in supporting your organization's software development goals to achieve consistent bottom-line improvements.

For a detailed presentation of my career background, please review the enclosed resume and feel free to contact me at your earliest convenience. Thank you in advance for your consideration and I look forward to speaking with you.

Best Regards,

King Lee

Project Management Professional Engineer—Direct Approach

To:

From:

Cc:

Subject: PMP Engineer

Dear [Name],

I am a Project Management Professional (PMP) engineer with extensive experience in manufacturing processes, quality control, supervision, and I lead multifunctional project teams from design to timely completion. My experience includes a history of progressive experience and increasing responsibilities.

As an engineer and project manager professional, I create value in a number of ways including:

- Establish and implement project management processes to ensure projects are delivered on time and within budget and scope.
- Use PMP methodologies to plan and manage scope, risk, cost, timelines, milestones, resources, and quality from initiation of the project through completion.
- Manage stakeholder expectations and provide clear status reports to management.
- Completed projects totaling over $1.6M.
- Research, design, and develop prototype mechanisms and manufacturing machinery.

I communicate effectively with all levels of the organization and with outside vendors and bring an outstanding work ethic, delivering high productivity in both team-oriented and self-directed environments. I take immense pride in delivering complex engineering projects.

I would like to talk with you to discuss how my skill set may match your clients' needs. I look forward to talking with you.

Sincerely,

[Your name]
[Your telephone number]

Project Manager—Direct Approach

To:

From:

Cc:

Subject: Project management

Dear [Name],

I heard through the professional grapevine that you might be looking for a Senior Project Manager and wanted to express interest and qualifications for such an opportunity. I am confident that my twelve years' experience with blue-chip technology giants will provide me with the necessary skills and frame of reference to make a meaningful contribution as a member of your team.

I specialize in the design, implementation, and continuous improvement of integrated marketing, operations, and training programs. Once parameters of responsibility are determined, I take command of a project, analyze the needs and means for desired outcomes, and deliver consistently problem-free and profitable results.

I would welcome the opportunity for a personal interview to further discuss my qualifications. I have attached my resume and can be reached at the above email or by phone at (817) 825-9452.

Sincerely,

Real Estate—Direct Approach

No one gets letters anymore, so they stand out and provide a break from the damn computer screen. Carole sent out ten of these letters in big envelopes so the resume lies flat. She had three phone calls within a week—one turned into her next gig.

CAROLE JENKINS

Melbourne & Los Angeles • 011 213-519-88-489 • commercialproperty@gmail.com

[Date]

[Name, Title]
[Company Name]
[Address]
[City, State Zip]

Dear [Name],

With a career of fifteen-plus years in the real estate industry, building a portfolio of successes within a variety of different environments and company structures, I offer the diverse experience, leadership, and skill that could benefit your organization.

➤ **A consistent record of success in analyzing, structuring, and executing transactions across multiple Asian property markets. In particular, I feel I can benefit investment houses operating in Asia with minimal exposure to managing institutional-grade properties in mature markets.**

➤ **The proven ability to lead asset management, property management, and leasing teams in meeting and exceeding objectives. I have collaborated with teams in acquiring over $1 billion in direct real estate.**

➤ **A portfolio of achievements that includes $650 million in underwriting, acquisition, and management, the establishment of the company's Jakarta branch office, the acquisition of 16 transactions valued at $42 million, and consistent 90%+ occupancy rates.**

Through my global experience, I have gained an in-depth awareness of cultural protocols and business practices in these regions that I have leveraged to achieve successful transactions and profitable asset/portfolio management. My list of contacts in Australia and China is extensive.

My resume will provide additional details concerning my qualifications and accomplishments. I would welcome the opportunity for an interview to discuss your organization's top needs and the performance you can expect from me. Thank you for your time and consideration.

Sincerely,

Carole Jenkins

Enclosure

Relocation for Application Developer

To:

From:

Cc:

Subject: Application Developer
_____

Dear [Name],

As an Application Developer I am very interested in joining your software development team. You have long been on my radar as a major innovator. You have a reputation for quality products, customer support, and being a great employer, and I want to work in an environment in which application development is critical.

My current position is Application Developer for _____. The job has provided me with 3 years' hands-on experience in Visual Basic and other languages. However, I am eager to jump into actual software writing, as well as return to the _____ area.

I have a Bachelor's Degree in Computer Science and am getting close to completing my Master's Degree.

My resume is attached for your review. I'll be back in _____ in three weeks, so I am going to call you to arrange a meeting for when I visit. In the meantime, please feel free to email or call for further information. Thank you for your consideration. I look forward to meeting you in the near future.

Yours truly,

(555) 555-1234

Research–Reference Librarian

To:
From:
Cc:
Subject: Research/Reference Librarian
_____

Dear [Name],

Are you looking for an **Entry-Level Research or Reference Librarian or Cataloguer**? My experience with Internet resources and navigational tools, combined with my experience with library databases, affords you the opportunity to hire an entry-level library professional with proven librarianship success.

With my recent MLIS, 3.95 from _____, as well as internship experience in the reference department of academic and state government libraries, perhaps I can be of service.

My resume is attached for your review; in it you will find information on my education, training, and work experience. I would like to draw your attention to credentials that are out of the norm:

- Fluent Polish, Russian, Slovak, German, Latin
- Taught English and Civics, pass rate of 100% over 8-year period: 2,000 foreign students
- Voyager Module, AACR2r, LC classification scheme, MARC format, and OCLC, as well as LexisNexis, Dow Jones, Dialog Web, and Classic

Providing high-level customer service and efficiency is my goal in library services. Can we meet soon to discuss your needs? I will call your office next week to schedule a mutually convenient appointment. Thank you for your time and consideration.

Sincerely,

(555) 555-1234

Sales and Marketing Strategist—Direct Approach

To:

From:

Cc:

Subject: Sales and Marketing Strategist

Dear [Name],

A forward-thinking company always requires self-directed professionals with proven leadership and business strategy skills. As a skilled Sales and Marketing Strategist, I would welcome the opportunity to discuss how my skills might contribute to your sales goals. I have:

- Surpassed financial goals and objectives, with $125 million in sales in one year.
- Established and created new marketing plans for product bulletins with a $5 million target.
- Surpassed sales targets by $1 million and increased margins by 5% in sales of ancillary products.
- Grown ancillary products margin 20% by sourcing globally.

With the ability to deftly navigate the challenges of today's extraordinary market conditions, I effectively link my skills and experience within the energy industry, leveraging a solid business acumen in account management, performance management, strategic planning, and relationship building. Plus I understand how to leverage technology as a competitive tool.

For a detailed presentation of my career background, please review the attached resume and then hopefully you will feel compelled to call me at the telephone number below my signature, or on the resume.

Best Regards,

(555) 555-1234

School Board Member

To:

From:

Cc:

Subject: School Board
_____

Dear [Name],

I am very interested in the vacated seat on the _____ City School Board. My motivation for seeking this position is public service. Because I have a deep commitment to community service and an in-depth knowledge of how a community works, I recognize that a public education system is critical to overall community success.

After retiring from law enforcement after thirty years of service, I returned to public service two years ago. I currently work as the Substance Abuse Prevention Coordinator for the City of _____ Health Department. Perspectives in the areas of substance abuse and public health would be beneficial to the school board.

In today's world, we fear for the security of our homeland. Our students and teachers need to be in a safe environment. Parents need to be confident that their children are secure at school and school-sponsored events. From my life experiences and training, I also bring expertise to the school board in this area.

Public service has always been my calling. An appointment to the _____ City School Board would allow me to use the skills gained from a 32-year career in public service to make a difference in people's lives. Though my children are grown, I look forward to a strong school system for my grand-children.

I have the time to devote to the task and the drive, energy, experience, and vision to make a positive contribution as a board member. I ask you to consider not only my qualifications but also my desire to serve. My extensive community involvement is outlined in the attached resume.

Sincerely,

(555) 555-1234

Senior Network Control Technician

To:

From:

Cc:

Subject: Senior Network Control Technician job posting

Dear [Name],

I am excited by your job posting for Senior Network Control Technician/Administrator. My qualifications and technical background, as well as fieldwork, marketing, and customer service experience, match your requirements for this position. The attached resume reflects the experience and technical training needed to provide customized network and hardware and software solutions to meet remote customer needs.

I believe the following are relevant to your needs:
- An accommodating attitude and willingness to work hard at any level to accomplish tasks and meet deadlines.
- The ability to multitask, prioritizing tasks and job assignments to balance customer needs with company goals.
- Strategic planning to head off downtime and restructure company systems to realize major improvement.
- Aptitude for troubleshooting problems, while respecting customers and explaining problems/solutions in accessible language.
- Consultative, straightforward communication techniques that promote development of strong and lasting rapport and trust.
- A work ethic that honors integrity and excellence to enhance company distinction.
- A persuasive, take-charge style seasoned with a sense of humor for a pleasant work environment.
- Psychological insight and a talent for motivating others to work at higher levels to increase productivity.

An interview to further investigate your needs and my qualifications would be of great interest to your clients. I look forward to hearing from you. Thank you for your time and consideration.

Sincerely,

(555) 555-1234

Strategic Sourcing Management—Direct Approach

To:

From:

Cc:

Subject: Strategic Sourcing Management

Dear [Name],

If you are interested in dramatically improving the performance and profitability of your organization, I would like to share my ideas with you. As a performance-focused leader with twenty years' experience in offshore manufacturing, I have a verifiable track record of accelerating growth through change, while significantly reducing costs to achieve world-class status and business sustainability.

I recently reduced costs through contract renegotiations while driving bottom line more than $1.5 million by expanding value proposition offerings while simultaneously creating a geographically disbursed vendor system.

One of my greatest strengths is in my ability to define and implement critical strategies to heighten revenue growth, reduce cost, and substantially improve overall customer service. For example, I increased revenue $.78 million by creating new systems to estimate production and fulfillment.

Capable of envisioning smart solutions to complex business issues, I also bring honed skills in collaborative leadership, communication, and flexibility. My past achievements are indicative of an effective leader who consistently gets results and leads energized teams.

I am ready to move to a new challenge in an arena where my unique skills and knowledge can bring immediate value and long-term superior solutions. I look forward to hearing from you to schedule an interview whereby I may learn more about your company's plans and goals and how I can contribute to its continued success.

Sincerely,

(555) 555-1234

Systems Performance—Direct Approach

To:

From:

Cc:

Subject: Systems Performance enhancement

Dear [Name],

Leading technology initiatives to drive systems performance, cut operational costs, and increase profitability is what I do best. Highlights of my qualifications include:

- Fifteen years' experience leading teams of highly skilled IT professionals in massive technology conversions and integrations projects
- Fifteen years' experience providing advanced technology solutions for regional hospitals and healthcare facilities
- MBA and BS in Management Information Systems
- Lean Six Sigma and Change Management Certifications

For the past seven years, I have worked as Director of Technology for ███████████████ ████████, where I provided strategic IT direction to bridge the gap between technology and business priorities and achieved extraordinary results. I can do the same for your company.

Let's schedule a time to meet to discuss how my technical project management skills might best serve your needs. I'm ready to talk as soon as you are. My number is below my signature.

Sincerely,

(555) 555-1234

Technology Conversion—Direct Approach

From: TechConversions@gmail.com

To: Recipient email address

Cc:

Subject: Hospital technology challenges

Dear [Name],

Technology integration and inevitable system-wide conversions are a massive headache—for everyone except me. Leading technology initiatives to drive systems performance, cut operational costs, and increase profitability is what I do best; it's my joy and my wheelhouse.

For the past seven years, I worked as Director of Technology for ███████████████████ ███████, where I provided strategic IT direction to bridge the gap between technology and business priorities and achieved extraordinary results. I am looking for a new challenge. Highlights of my qualifications include:

- MBA and BS in Management Information Systems
- Lean Six Sigma and Change Management Certifications
- Twelve years' experience providing advanced technology solutions for regional hospitals and healthcare facilities and leading teams of highly skilled IT professionals in massive technology conversions and integrations projects

I can fix system integration, upgrades, and conversions causing trauma in your hospitals. Would it make sense to talk about the challenges and the solutions? My resume is attached and my number is below.

Sincerely,

[Your name]
[Your telephone number]

Veterinarian

To:
From:
Cc:
Subject: Veterinarian

Dear [Name],

My 15 years' experience addressing the health and performance needs of race horses at major tracks make me a strong candidate for the opening you recently advertised at the AAEP website. Accordingly, I have attached my resume for your consideration and review.

Some key points include:

Strong capacity to function independently and make critical decisions without direct supervision. My knowledge of horses and experience at several major tracks means that I will need minimal orientation to "hit the ground running."

An excellent track record maintaining the health of thoroughbreds and quarter horses, as well as assisting trainers in enhancing the performance of horses by improving their respiratory and general health and dealing with lameness issues (references can be provided).

The ability to effectively evaluate young horses prior to purchase, through observation and diagnostic testing. I routinely produce quality repository radiographs and review radiographs in a repository setting. I also accompany buyers to auctions (Keeneland, etc.) to assess horses under consideration.

Experience assisting trainers setting up effective farm-based training programs, as well as helping breeders address reproductive health issues for horses in breeding farm settings.

I believe that I can be an asset to your organization, and would enjoy discussing further how my knowledge, expertise, and professional dedication can address your needs. Please feel free to contact me to arrange either a phone or in-person interview at a mutually convenient date and time.

Thank you for your time and consideration. I look forward to speaking with you.

Sincerely,

[Your name]
[Your telephone number]
Attachment: resume

Vice President of Asset Liquidation

To:

From:

Cc:

Subject: Asset liquidation assignment? Get this guy!

_____

Dear [Name],

As the Vice President of Lease Asset Liquidation with _____, I successfully engineered the recovery of $23 million in assets, almost three times the original buyout offer of $8 million.

Throughout my career I have been instrumental in developing and implementing workout and liquidation strategies and have earned a strong reputation as a professional who gets the job done.

My reason for contacting you is simple. I am interested in project opportunities that will serve both to challenge and to utilize my abilities in asset liquidation management. My current project will be completed within the next four to six weeks. I am currently considering offers and intend to make a decision by February 1st.

Please see my attached resume for details. I look forward to hearing from you to discuss any mutually beneficial opportunities.

Sincerely,

(555) 555-1234

LETTERS TO HEADHUNTERS

Applications Development—Headhunter

To:

From:

Cc:

Subject: Applications Development—Headhunter cover

Dear [Name],

Do you have a client seeking a Director of Applications Development with experience leading large-scale IT initiatives for the design, development, and implementation of advanced applications for MIS and POS systems in the retail sector? If so, this is what I do best: Create IT solutions to drive retail operations performance, cut costs, and increase profitability.

My qualifications include:

- MBA with an IT Focus and BS in Management Information Systems.
- Fifteen years' experience in the IT industry creating computer applications to allow big-picture analysis and detailed financial reporting for a global retail chain with annual revenues exceeding $1.6 billion.
- Twelve years' management and leadership experience with computer systems analysts, computer programmers, business analysts, and help desk technicians.

As Manager of Application Development for Retail Systems with ▓▓▓▓ I manage a $1 million software budget and have created applications to bridge the gap between technology and business priorities with impressive results—even if I say so myself ;-).

Can we schedule a meeting to discuss ways in which my leadership, technical, and managerial strengths can be of service to one of your clients? My telephone number is below my signature.

Sincerely,

(555) 555-1234

Construction Management—Headhunter

To:
From:
Cc:
Subject: Construction Management searches?

Dear [Name],

I am in the construction management and business management fields and am writing to follow up on a resume I sent last week: Name: John Smith, Target Job: Construction Management. I have attached my resume to the end of this email in case the above-mentioned resume has gone missing.

I am looking for a management position that leverages the experience and abilities reflected in the attached resume. If any positions become available, I would be happy to discuss the details. Thanks for your consideration. I'll call in a couple of days to follow up.

Sincerely,

(555) 555-1234

Global Consulting—Headhunter

To:
From:
Cc:
Subject: Global Consulting

Dear [Name],

I am an advisory client services management professional for a global consulting firm with extensive experience in identifying and leading the development and implementation of industry-specific business processes to improve productivity, quality, operating performance, and profitability for a wide variety of Fortune 500 clients across diverse industries.

I deliver positive results for clients in a number of ways, for example:

- Developed agenda for three new CFOs to help with prioritizing initiatives, evaluating direct reports' deliverables and performance, and created plans to help guide their first 180 days in office.
- Developed strategy for CFO and finance department to reduce costs and improve efficiency through a shared service center, improved treasury operations, and reporting.
- Designed and executed process improvements for annual and long-range strategic planning processes aligning financial planning with operational forecasts; reduced planning cycle by two months.
- Assisted client struggling with Sarbanes-Oxley demands. Implemented internal control and compliance programs focused on PCAOB and SEC compliance, preventing client's stock from being delisted.

My leadership skills, coupled with my technical know-how, enable me to consistently coach client management through successful implementation of business strategies. I relate well with all organizational levels, including acting as the primary contact for C-level executives during project implementations. I take pride in delivering quality engagements.

I would like to talk with you to discuss how my skill set may match a client's needs. I look forward to talking with you.

Sincerely,

(555) 555-1234

Life Science—Headhunter

To:

From:

Cc:

Subject: Life Science Finance assignments

Dear [Name]:

I have identified your search firm as having strong contacts within the high-growth Life Sciences organizations. My strengths include a successful track record in medical science and business. I am currently employed at the ████ Clinic, where I develop solutions to link medical expertise with business goals and the financial strategies that deliver them.

My experience combined with my academic background gives me a unique understanding of research and the impacts on business strategies. I have a BS in Bioengineering and in Finance.

I would like to talk with you to discuss how my skill set may match your clients' needs. I look forward to talking with you and can be reached at the number below.

Sincerely,

(555) 555-1234

Restaurant Franchise Management—Headhunter

To:

From:

Cc:

Subject: Restaurant Franchise management

Dear [Name]:

I am a restaurant management professional with nineteen years' experience directing successful business operations, and a designated troubleshooter for troubled operations and start-ups. I currently hold the position of General Manager for a franchisee of eleven full-service dining franchises.

As general manager, I am responsible for overseeing every aspect of restaurant operations, including recruitment, employee training and development, budgeting, accounting, sales forecasting, payroll, inventory, and scheduling. Obviously I am accomplished at working in fast-paced environments with heavy demands while providing consistent customer satisfaction.

As a general manager, I create value in a number of ways including:

- Ensure company initiatives are executed with a maximum profitability by minimizing operational costs.
- Establish and implement employee cross-training programs, resulting in a reduction in labor costs by 18%.
- Improved guest experience ratings from 42% to 63% in less than six months.
- Reduced food waste from 18% to 5% in six months.
- Improved overall performance, earning restaurant $250,000 annually for three consecutive years.
- Instrumental in the turnaround of underperforming restaurants and numerous start-ups.
- Mentor general managers to assist new and existing restaurant operation excellence.

I take pride in managing high-performance restaurants and consistently delivering high productivity and excellent customer service. I would like to talk with you to discuss how my skill set may match your client's need. I look forward to talking with you and can be reached at (404) 555-1234.

Sincerely,

[Name]

FOLLOW-UP LETTERS

401(k) Professional

To:
From:
Cc:
Subject: James/Culbertson Communications Consultant meeting

Dear [Name],

It was very enjoyable to speak with you about the Communications Consultant position last Wednesday, January 11th. I truly appreciate all the time and care you took in exploring the scope of responsibilities and examining my qualifications.

I will bring my Section 401(k) experience to bear with good effect—directing the brand communications experience from initial conception through execution; positioning strong development, execution, and management experience of 401(k) plan marketing and communication strategies for plan sponsors, plan participants, financial consultants, and investment committees; thoughtfully managing resources and budgets in alignment with overarching communication plans and goals.

I am comfortable interacting with all levels of internal and external clientele, including Client Relationship Managers, Chief Financial Officers, Human Resources Directors, and Investment Committees, one-on-one or during a boardroom presentation.

I always strive to create trust and respect; building solid relationships across an organization and with key external constituencies has always been an essential ingredient in my overall success as a leader.

I am excited about this opportunity and eager to move forward.

Sincerely,

(555) 555-1234

CEO Personal Assistant

To:
From:
Cc:
Subject: CEO's P/A interview follow-up
_____

Dear [Name],

The time I spent interviewing with you and _____ this afternoon gave me a clear picture of your company's operation as well as your corporate environment. I want to thank you, in particular, _____, for the thorough picture you painted of your CEO's needs and work style.

I left our meeting feeling very enthusiastic about the scope of the position as well as its close match to my abilities and work style. After reviewing your comments, I think the key strengths that I can offer your CEO in achieving his agenda are:

- Experience in effectively dealing with senior-level staff in a manner that facilitates decision-making.
- Proven ability to anticipate an executive's needs and present viable options to consider.
- Excellent communication skills—particularly the ability to gain feedback from staff and summarize succinctly.

Whether the needs at hand involve meeting planning, office administration, scheduling, or executive access, I bring a combination of highly effective "people skills" and diversified business experience to deal with changing situations.

With my energetic work style, I believe that I am an excellent match for this unique position. I would welcome an additional meeting to elaborate on my background and how I can assist your CEO. I am excited; when can we talk again?

Sincerely,

(555) 555-1234

Director of Plant Services

To:

From:

Cc:

Subject: Glad we finally caught up RE: Director of Physical Plant Services

Dear [Name],

I appreciate the time you took yesterday to discuss the Physical Plant Services job. I recognize that timing and awareness of interest are very important in searches of this type.

Your comment regarding an attempt to contact me earlier this summer is a case in point, but an ailing parent trumps all. Because of the situation, I wouldn't have been any good at an interview anyway. Now I am loaded for bear.

Attached, as you requested, you will find my resume. My experiences as a Director of Physical Plant Services are readily transferable to new environments; the horizontal flexibility is one of the appeals of the job.

You can reach me by email or telephone. I look forward to hearing from you. Thank you for your time and consideration.

Sincerely,

(555) 555-1234

Entry-Level Pension Fund Administrator

To:
From:
Cc:
Subject: Thank you for the meeting
_____

Dear [Name],

I would like to take this opportunity to thank you for the interview this Wednesday morning, and to confirm my strong interest in an entry-level Customer Service position with the _____ department.

As we discussed, I feel that a BA and an internship with a pension fund have provided me with an understanding of the basic business operations and will help me quickly prove to be an asset. Additionally, I have always been considered a hard worker and a dependable, loyal employee. I am confident that I can make a valuable contribution to your Group Pension Fund area.

I look forward to meeting with you again in the near future to take the next steps. I am sincerely interested and enthusiastic about the position.

Sincere regards,

(555) 555-1234

Executive Assistant Follow-Up

From: ExecRightHand@earthlink.net

To:

Cc:

Subject: Recent meeting

Dear [Name],

I enjoyed our conversation on Friday; I appreciated your feedback, regarding the executive assistant position, and learning more about the culture at ██.

To answer your question about my ability to work under pressure: My previous boss was affectionately known by everyone as TD, for Tasmanian Devil; she never stopped and was proud of it. I was hired because she wanted a trustworthy, super competent assistant who could adapt to her high-speed pace and always look out for her best interests. So yes, I thrive in fast-paced, deadline-driven environments.

I understand the responsibilities on your plate, as National Vice President, Platform Solutions Group reporting to the CEO; gate-keeping, organizing, planning, scheduling on- and off-site meetings, heavy calendaring across multiple time zones are all second nature to me. As a top-level EA, I will provide you with my full support 24/7! With my careful attention to detail, concerns about streamlining daily operations will evaporate with me in the saddle.

You know what you need, and from my experience, that is half the battle. I can deliver the other half . . . delivering services such as expense and sales reports, tracking and monitoring expenses, and arranging travel that you need to confidently delegate so that you can focus on making ██ the most profitable it can be.

Thank you for your time and for this exciting opportunity! I believe we could make a formidable team.

Sincerely,

[Your name]
[Your telephone number]

Fundraising Consultant

To:
From:
Cc:
Subject: Re: Fundraising Consultant meeting
_____

Dear [Name],

Thank you for making time to explore how I could help _____ as your newest Fundraising Consultant.

I've already starting thinking about how I might be most productive—right from the start. Of course, my ideas must be preliminary; I don't know nearly enough about how your organization works. Nevertheless, in response to your observations, I would value your reactions to these preliminary thoughts:

* Clients need to see the tailored solutions we provide as a rapid, seamless, continuing operation that guides them through the complex world of modern fundraising.

* Position and brand the company as the "sole source" for the resources they must have to grow financially and operationally.

I am modifying my continuing professional development program to concentrate on fundraising from a consultant's perspective; this is where I see the future. I am looking through the literature and contacting my network to learn their feelings about working with fundraising consultants today.

I'll use what I learn to reevaluate my own successes in campaigns done with and without consultants. I think this current competitive analysis, and my frame of reference from the "other side of the street," could be of value in strategic planning for our marketing initiatives.

I appreciate your vote of confidence in recommending that I meet with _____ _____.
I want to make that interview just as useful for her as possible. Toward that end, may I call in a few days to get your reactions to the preliminary thoughts I've outlined above?

With many thanks for all your help . . .

Sincerely,

(555) 555-1234

Headhunter—Initial Phone Interview Follow-Up

To:
From:
Cc:
Subject: Candidate for quantitative analysis, investment analysis, risk management

Dear [Name],

Thank you for taking time to speak with me today. Your firm's reputation within the investment management industry prompted my call, and I am happy to learn that you have an active search that might fit my profile.

Working as a Quantitative Analyst at ████████ over the past four years, I have gained valuable experience and solid skills that may be an asset, especially with a client such as ██████████:

* Strong background in growth, value, and quantitative investment strategies.
* Experience in measuring portfolios against various benchmarks.
* Polished communication skills with portfolio managers.
* Quantitative risk control of portfolios.
* Passion for markets and for finding investment solutions for institutional clients.

To focus my skills in quantitative investment analysis, I recently graduated with an MS in Financial Mathematics.

I look forward to hearing from you about this and other suitable opportunities.

Sincerely,

(555) 555-1234

Headhunter—Phone Follow-Up

To:
From:
Cc:
Subject: Jane's prediction was right! Great meeting.

Dear [Name],

Thank you for meeting with me this morning. Our mutual friend, Jane Topper, assured me that a meeting with you would be productive, and it was. I sincerely appreciate your counsel, insight, and advice.

I have attached my resume for your review. I would appreciate any feedback you may have regarding effectiveness and strength. I understand you may not have any searches under way that would be suitable for me at this time, but I would appreciate any future considerations.

As we reviewed this morning, I seek and am qualified for senior MIS positions in a medium to large high-tech manufacturing or services business. I seek compensation in the $150,000 and above range, and look to report directly to the C-suite. These requirements are intelligently flexible depending on all the obvious factors. My family and I are willing to relocate to any area except [place names].

Thanks again and please let me know if I can be of service to you in any related searches in my area of expertise; I'm always happy to suggest a referral. I have learned how important networking is. I really appreciate your assistance and wish to reciprocate.

Sincerely,

(555) 555-1234

HR, T&D, Distance Learning

To:
From:
Cc:
Subject: Follow-up, today's 3 P.M. Distance Learning meeting

Dear [Name],

Thank you very much for taking the time to meet with me today. I enjoyed our discussion, and I'm excited about the possibilities inherent in joining your team.

It was great to learn that you are embracing learning technology tools as they relate to the HR and T&D function—both in terms of day-to-day operations and the future delivery of company training programs (e.g., distance learning) to a dispersed client base.

I am very interested in, and have an affinity for, integrating technology into the HR function and then into the day-to-day operations of the company, and would love to be a part of your efforts in this area.

As we established, I have related experience in all of the required areas for the position. Establishing the new system for the delivery of the assessment workshops to your key clients would be an exciting kick-off project, and one that recent experience predicts I will ace in short order.

I am very interested in the position, and I look forward to hearing from you soon. If you require additional information in the meantime, I may be reached at (555) 555-1234.

Sincerely,

(555) 555-1234

Library Development

To:
From:
Cc:
Subject: Monday afternoon's Librarian selection meeting

Dear [Name],

Thank you for the opportunity to meet with you and the selection committee on Monday afternoon at 4 HE. I enjoyed our discussion of the Associate State Librarian for Library Development opening and I was impressed with the panel's vision for this role.

Based on our conversation, I believe that I possess the capabilities to successfully meet your expectations for this key position with the State Library.

To reiterate the experiences I bring to this position, please note the following:

- Promoting programs and fostering working relationships with over 1,000 member libraries in all major segments of the field. These activities also encompass extensive community outreach.
- Providing strategic vision and mission, and motivating staff to pursue organizational goals. In countless assignments, I have recognized member library staffs for their focused efforts in ways that have delivered exceptional program results.
- Managing capital projects and spearheading information technology initiatives. These encompassed upgrades to comply with ADA access requirements, renovations that improved space utilization, and leading efforts to incorporate technology into library settings.
- Supervising departments in urban and suburban settings to address a broad range of competing priorities. Among these experiences was the supervision of an Interlibrary Loan department serving 100 individual branches in a five-county area.

I am most interested in this position and am confident that my track record at _____ demonstrates my capacity to "hit the ground running" and apply my leadership, enthusiasm, and expertise to furthering the mission of state libraries in this development role. I look forward to continuing our discussions in the near future.

Sincerely,

(555) 555-1234

Logistics Management Follow-Up

To:
From:
Cc:
Subject: Logistics management candidate

Dear [Name],

It was a pleasure talking with you yesterday at 4 P.M. in reference to the Logistics position with ███████████. I appreciate the time you spent with me, as well as the valuable insights you offered. As you suggested, I have adjusted my resume to reflect more accurately my relevant skills for this job and have attached the new version so that your files can be updated.

Thank you again for the compliment on my ability to deliver a strong interview. Please keep this in mind when considering me for placement with one of your clients. If I can be of assistance with other searches in my field, please let me know; in twelve years, I've gotten to know a lot of people.

Sincerely,

[Your name]
[Your telephone number]

Manufacturer's Representative

From:

To:

Cc:

Subject: Our Manufacturer's Representative meeting

Dear [Name],

Thank you for allowing me to interview with you on Friday, February 23rd for the Manufacturer's Representative position. Everything I learned from you about _____ leads me to believe that this is a progressive company where I could fully utilize my skills and make a valuable contribution. In fact, I have not been this determined or excited about a job since I started my career twenty years ago.

As I mentioned to you, I am sales oriented and have a solid technical background in printing. I relate well to printers at any level, from press people to owners. In my sales activities with _____ _____, when he was a printing buyer at _____, I found him to be very demanding and hard to please. One of the reasons why I was successful in acquiring and retaining his business was my constant commitment to customer service. Whenever there were any questions, I never failed to answer them promptly.

During our discussion, you seemed to express a concern about my lack of experience with dealers. I have had long-term relationships with dealers like _____, and have bought approximately $1 million worth of equipment from them, starting with my first press and expanding to twenty over the years. I am certain that with my persistence and follow-through, I can handle dealers at the sales and service end.

Among my major strengths, I am goal-driven, self-motivated, have a strong work ethic, and an ability to learn quickly. My training period would be brief, and I would use my own time to familiarize myself with your equipment and product line. In addition, I am accustomed to long hours and have no objection to the travel requirements throughout the Middle Atlantic States or being away from home four days a week.

Coming from a medium-sized company, it would be an honor to work at _____. I look forward to talking further about my candidacy.

Sincerely,

(555) 555-1234

Mental Health Senior Counselor

To:
From:
Cc:
Subject: Looking forward to next week

Dear [Name],

I would like to thank you for affording me the opportunity to meet with you to discuss the Senior Counselor position with your organization. I have long been an admirer of your services and commitment to the community. I am very confident that my education, experience, and counseling skills will enable me to make an immediate and long-term contribution to your mental health program.

The position we discussed seems well suited to my strengths and skills, because both my counseling and teaching backgrounds include a real emphasis on the family unit and its influence and relationship to each client's therapy.

I genuinely am looking forward to seeing you again next week; it is so stimulating to discuss the needs of our calling with someone similarly committed and with such a tremendous frame of reference. If you require any additional information before then, please feel free to call.

Sincerely,

(555) 555-1234

Operations Management Follow-Up

To:
From:
Cc:
Subject: Operations Management pro, thanks for the conversation

---

Dear [Name],

Thank you for allowing me to tell you a little about myself this morning. Here are some further details as requested:

Ten years' operations management experience; the ABILITY to quickly understand, manage, and build business; EXPERIENCE in domestic and international corporate cultures; INTELLIGENCE and the capacity to grasp essential elements; and the WILLINGNESS to work hard, travel, and relocate.

I have just completed my MBA and would appreciate the opportunity to talk with client companies that are in need of my substantial background in operational management, marketing, and technical products.

I'm not necessarily looking for fancy titles (but I am promotable). What I am looking for is that special position that will offer not only a challenge but also an opportunity with long-range potential.

I will be happy to discuss details with you once you have reviewed the attached resume. May we work together?

Sincerely,

[Your name]
[Your telephone number]

Senior Executive Assistant

To:

From:

Cc:

Subject: Senior Executive Assistant Meeting

Dear [Name],

I want to express my appreciation to you and your team for the time and courtesy extended to me during my interview on _____ . I enjoyed the discussions and am even more enthusiastic about the Senior Executive Assistant position at _____ .

I recognize the importance of the Senior Executive Assistant's role, and based on my past successes I am confident that I can meet the challenge. My educational background is strong and includes an MBA degree with a major in Marketing, plus many hours of continuing professional education.

Likewise, my work experience and skills in administrative duties, calendar management, budgeting, data management, risk management, and research and planning would permit me to make some valuable contributions to your team. Specifully, my experience includes:

- Ability to anticipate the executive's needs and proactively bring together resources to support executive in addressing issues.
- Facility for working effectively with people at all levels of management and cross-functional teams on a global basis.
- High level of confidentiality, professionalism, and sound judgment.
- Processing new hires, plus employee training and development.
- Experience in administration, general management, and presentations.
- Proven ability to generate fresh ideas and creative solutions to difficult problems.
- Ability to successfully manage multiple projects in fast-paced environments.

I was impressed by the warm and confident professionalism of your team and look forward to moving our conversations forward to their logical conclusion. I am excited about the opportunity and I want to join the team as your next Senior Executive Assistant. Please do not hesitate to contact me at (555) 555-1234 or emailaddress@yourserver.net.

Sincerely,

(555) 555-1234

Wholesale Market Manager Follow-Up

To:

From:

Cc:

Subject: Yesterday's Market Management interview

Dear [Name],

Thank you for meeting me yesterday in relation to the Wholesale Market Manager opening. I understand that the search is continuing and would like to ask that, as an early candidate, you keep my accomplishments and the success of our interview in mind:

- Direct experience in all phases of wholesale commercial banking, including: market segmentation, prospecting, building and maintaining customer relationships, lending, and the sale of noncredit products and services.

- Captured a 24% share of public funds market within two years, and captured a 22% share of insurance company funds market.

- Developed cash management and trust products tailored to the needs of my target market; $55 million in sales in three years.

- Marketed services through email, social networking, investor-specific seminars, and through active participation in target market's industry professional organizations.

I will call you next week, after you have seen the other candidates, to continue our discussion. In the meantime, please be assured of my competency and commitment.

Sincerely,

[Your name]
[Your telephone number]

NETWORKING LETTERS

Adult Education Networking

To:

From:

Cc:

Subject: Thanks for the referral

Dear [Name],

Good to talk to you yesterday. As requested during our telephone conversation I'm attaching my resume for the Adjunct Adult Education position currently available. I appreciate your offer to forward these credentials to the hiring manager.

With a Master's degree in Education Administration, and Administration and Supervision certifications through the state of Maine, plus four years of cumulative experience in the classroom, I possess the hands-on expertise and educational credentials that are critical to guiding adult students in pursuit of their educational goals.

What do I offer [Name] Community College students?

- Effective listening and communication skills—a demonstrated ability to provide the individualized instruction based on students' interests and needs.
- Encouragement and motivation—an empowering atmosphere of interaction and participation.
- Sincere desire to reach each student on a level s/he can understand, no matter the skill level or cultural background.

I am excited by the opportunity to work with adult students, because the adult population brings a unique flavor of enthusiasm and motivation that energizes and inspires me as an instructor.

My resume is attached and I would welcome the opportunity to talk further. Thank you for your consideration.

Sincerely,

[Your name]
[Your telephone number]

Animation Technology, Networking

To:

From:

Cc:

Subject: Harry Jones with more on animation technology

_____

Dear [Name],

Moshimoshi. Since meeting earlier this year at the Korean Film Festival we have exchanged emails and met several times. We have discussed our mutual interest in the Japanese movie industry and its future in the global entertainment business. You know well my vision of integrating Japanese gaming and animation technologies into filmmaking.

Over the course of our conversations, you mentioned that there might be an opportunity for an internship or, possibly, employment at _____. I am very interested.

I offer negotiation, persuasion, and liaison abilities, plus leadership and communication skills. I have also proven that I can use my bilingual proficiency to enhance business understanding. Please see my attached resume for examples of how I have used these abilities in the past.

I believe that my unique strengths can contribute to the growth of the _____ program, particularly if you are able to secure departmental status. I welcome the opportunity to discuss my continued involvement in your program.

Sincerely,

(555) 555-1234

Big Data Networking

To:

From:

Cc:

Subject: 6 Years intranet implementation 15K users

Dear [Name],

Our mutual friend Carole Anderson mentioned that you are looking for a Database Administrator with experience big data and cloud management.

As she described the job, it sounded exactly like the kind of work I can sink my teeth into. I would welcome the opportunity to discuss my expertise in relation to the specific deliverables of your job.

I have done exactly this kind of work for the past seven years, and as my company has an imminent merger I am looking to make a change. Carole suggested that I send you the attached resume.

Would you take a look at it and if you see some synergy perhaps we can we talk—my number is below my signature,

Sincerely,

(555) 555-1234

Common Background and Interests—Networking

To:

From:

Cc:

Subject: Jack Sykes asked me to say hi

Dear [Name],

John Sykes at GM says hello and suggested I contact you after commenting that my background, business philosophy, and style reminded him of a CEO he had heard speak in Houston last year—apparently you were the hit of the conference.

I am a V.P. of Operations who, like you, started on the shop floor and worked my way up through the ranks from Foreman, to Plant Supervisor, to Manufacturing Engineer, to Director of Operations, and finally Vice President of Operations, taking a swing at every new idea that came my way. I may have missed a few, but overall my batting average has been good. Three examples:

- Led a $340M manufacturing firm to earning ISO9002 certification on first attempt.
- Increased productivity at a plant in Mexico 34%, and reduced downtime 17%.
- Increased profits by 200% by restructuring production and delivery logistics.

I believe strongly in teams and am cross-functionally effective working with R&D, engineering, and marketing units to achieve corporate goals. My colleagues have expressed appreciation for my direct and honest approach to people and problems.

Between jobs now, I am off on a fishing trip for Tarpon (I hear you are a sport fisherman too). I will be in Miami next week, and if you have time I would like to get together for lunch or coffee as time permits. I will give you a call tomorrow morning to see if that can be arranged.

Please see my attached resume for a comprehensive picture of my professional background. I look forward to meeting you.

Sincerely,

[Your name]
[Your telephone number]

Construction Management, Networking

To:
From:
Cc:
Subject: Follow-up on Chamber of Commerce conversation

Dear [Name],

We had the opportunity to speak briefly at the Chamber of Commerce meeting last week about the Construction Management position you are seeking to fill in ___. I appreciate you filling me in on the details of the project, and I'm following up as you suggested.

As we discussed, I am well acquainted with ___'s brand and store concept, and I am excited to learn of your expansion plans. With my background in construction, maintenance, project management, and operations leadership, I believe I am primed to play a key role in this growth.

As the founder of Superior Landscape Design, I have been instrumental in leading the company to phenomenal success within a very short time, building the organization from start-up into a solid revenue generator reputed throughout the Pacific Northwest as an aggressive competitor in markets crowded by multi-million-dollar, nationally recognized companies.

I am currently in the process of selling the company, and have been exploring opportunities with dynamic, growth-oriented organizations like yours that could benefit from my broad-based expertise in operations, organizational management, finance, and business development. Complementing my diverse leadership background is expertise in all the fundamentals of construction management, including the ability to see projects through to completion on time and on budget.

Perhaps one of my strongest assets is my ability to cultivate long-lasting relationships with clients through attentive, direct communication. I have been highly successful at defining complex project plans, establishing budgets, outlining scope of work, and directly soliciting qualified contractors utilizing the bid process. I also offer extensive experience navigating paperwork and bureaucracy, through which I forge productive alliances with key regulatory agencies to streamline permitting and licensing and expedite project starts.

I would enjoy the opportunity to speak with you again in greater detail. Could we meet for lunch on Friday? I have enclosed my resume and will call your assistant in a few days to confirm a meeting.

Sincerely,

(555) 555-1234

Cross-Functional Networking

To:

From:

Cc:

Subject: Sincere thanks for the help ;-)

Dear [Name],

Thank you for making the time to meet with me for coffee yesterday. It was fascinating to learn about the ways data-mining technology is being applied to the creation of mammoth academic eLibraries; we live in exciting times.

Given my background in data management this opened up a new professional horizon for me that connects my professional skills with my personal obsessions for learning. I will be contacting Dr. Khiem Jackson as you suggested and will let you know how things are progressing once I have made the connection.

I am grateful for the time you took out of your busy schedule to assist me in my job search. Please, if you have any additional thoughts—I'm all ears for your wisdom.

Thanks again for your help. You will be hearing from me soon.

Sincerely,

(555) 555-1234

Designer—Networking

To:

From:

Cc:

Subject: Let's keep in touch

Dear [Name],

It was a pleasure speaking with you yesterday afternoon. Thanks for your help regarding my search for a position in Corporate Graphic Design.

The position I am looking for is usually found in a corporate marketing or public relations department. The titles vary: Design Manager, Advertising Manager, and Publications Director are a few. In almost every case the job description includes the production and distribution of the corporation's online and print marketing materials.

If you run into anyone connected to my professional areas of expertise, my portfolio documents over eight years of experience in the business and includes design, project consultation, and supervision of quality printed material for a wide range of clients.

If I come across anyone suitable to your needs, I'll certainly give you a shout. Let's keep in touch.

Sincerely,

(555) 555-1234

Education Administration, Networking

To:
From:
Cc:
Subject: Thanks for the referral

Dear [Name],

I enclose my resume as requested during our telephone conversation yesterday afternoon regarding the Adjunct Adult Education position currently available. I appreciate your offer to forward these credentials to Ms. _____ _____.

With a Master's Degree in Education Administration, and a Principal of Administration and Supervision certification through the state of _____, plus four years of cumulative experience in the classroom, I possess the hands-on expertise and educational credentials that are critical to guiding adult students in pursuit of their educational goals.

What do I offer _____ Community College students?

- Effective listening and communication skills—a demonstrated ability to provide individualized instruction based on students' interests and needs.
- Encouragement and motivation—an empowering atmosphere of interaction and participation.
- Sincere desire to reach each student on a level s/he can understand, no matter the skill level or cultural background.

I am excited at the opportunity to work with adult students, because I recognize that they are in that classroom because they want to be there. The adult population brings a unique flavor of enthusiasm and motivation that energizes and inspires me as an instructor.

My resume is attached for forwarding to _____ _____. I would welcome the opportunity for an interview to discuss this job and a place on your educational team. Thank you for your consideration.

Sincerely,

(555) 555-1234

EMEA Marketing Administration—Networking

To:

From:

Cc:

Subject: EMEA Marketing Administration

Dear [Name],

Yang Chi suggested that I contact you in regard to your need for an EMEA Marketing Administrator. I have three years' experience in office administration, customer service, sales, training, and marketing for EMEA-focused operations, and my German and French fluency will be an asset with your European business.

My resume is attached for your review. Highlights include:

☑ I consistently focus on creating and maintaining excellent client relationships, and training others in successful techniques to do the same.

☑ A resourceful problem solver with a track record of getting positive results, such as a 75% collection rate on accounts ninety days past due.

☑ Ability to build confidence and trust at all levels, and demonstrated experience in supporting cooperative, results-oriented environments.

☑ Proven communication skills, including fluency in French and German.

My career success has been due in large part to supporting teams, as well as internal and external customer relationships, and tackling persistent problem areas with creative approaches.

If my qualifications meet with your needs, which I believe they will, I would be available to schedule a meeting immediately. Thank you for your consideration. I look forward to hearing from you.

Sincerely,

(555) 555-1234

Finance and Social Connections

To:

From:

Cc:

Subject: Be thankful you're not me Charlie ;-)

Hi Charlie,

Just found an original Thurston Iasia. What a poster! The colors are still really fresh! Sadly can't justify the expense right now—c'est la guerre! You interested?

Hope all is well with you and yours and that you aren't going through the upheaval of job change like I am. I am no longer with Citigroup and am actively seeking my next career opportunity.

Would you take a look at Ye Olde resume, which is attached—actually it's all new and up-to-date—and advise me of any options/avenues you think I should explore? Names of Director/CP/C-level guys would be much appreciated. Maybe there is someone among your friends or colleagues with whom I could speak?

I hope you'll scratch your head for me. If anything comes to mind, please let me know. Thanks in advance for your thoughts and I'll give you a call next week, if for nothing more than to catch up on your poster collection. No pressure on this, Charlie, just help if you can. I welcome any advice/input/support/kick in the pants and look forward to returning the favor immediately or at any time in the future.

Sincerely,

(555) 555-1234

Financial Professional, Networking

To:
From:
Cc:
Subject: _____ suggested I contact you re Finance Associate position
_____

Dear [Name],

I recently spoke with ____ _____ from _____ _____, and he strongly recommended that I send you a copy of my resume. I am very pleased to learn of the need for a **Finance Associate** and I believe the qualities you seek are well matched by my track record:

Your Needs	My Qualifications
3–5 years of experience building and maintaining complex financial models	Four years of experience at a top-performing hedge fund
	Built and maintained complex financial models to support investment theses in private equity transactions and coverage of over 30 stocks, $100M of portfolio value
	Created matrices in Excel to analyze model sensitivity to risk factors
Background of exceptional academic performance	BS in Economics with Honors from _____
Ability to manage multiple projects and meet deadlines	Delivered 15–20 research reports and notes per month in a fast-paced work environment

My greatest strength lies in my ability to clearly communicate complex financial information. This has enabled me to summarize the results of models and in-depth due diligence into concise investment theses for the portfolio managers of ____ _____, resulting in many profitable investments.

I am confident that my dedication, enthusiasm, and creativity would allow me to make a real contribution to your team. I hope to speak with you further and will call the week of August 2nd to follow up with you. Hopefully you'll be so fired up by the attached resume that you'll call or email me sooner.

Sincerely,

(555) 555-1234

Gaming Industry—Networking

To:

From:

Cc:

Subject: Future of gaming

Dear [Name],

Since meeting earlier this year at the London Film Festival we have exchanged emails and discussed our mutual interest in animation and its growing role in the future of the global entertainment business.

Last time we talked, you mentioned that there might be an opportunity in business development at your company. I want you to know that I am very interested.

Please see my attached resume for examples of how I have used negotiation, persuasion, and liaison abilities, plus leadership, and communication skills to instigate and negotiate distribution deals—often using my bilingual proficiency to enhance understanding.

If you could pass this on to the appropriate party, and perhaps give me a name and email address so I can follow up, it would be much appreciated.

Your friend,

(555) 555-1234

Local Services, Networking

To:

From:

Cc:

Subject: Thanks for the advice

Dear [Name],

Congratulations on your reelection. I hope this letter finds you and your family well, and that you are having an enjoyable holiday season.

I am writing to update you on my job search. You may recall from our last conversation that I am now focusing on obtaining an hourly position with basic benefits that will sustain me until such time as I am ready for retirement (in three to five years).

As you recommended, I have applications on file with the Town of _____ for various positions, and have corresponded with various department heads, in each case indicating my flexibility and strong interest in making a meaningful contribution to smooth operations within one of their departments.

_____, I genuinely appreciate the advice and assistance you have offered to date. Once again, I am requesting that if you are aware of any other avenues I should be pursuing, please forward the attached resume and let me know.

I believe I have skills and experience to offer and can be an asset to someone in just about any position requiring maturity, reliability, and dedication. Thank you, again, for all your help, and Merry Christmas.

Sincerely,

(555) 555-1234

Networking at Church

To:

From:

Cc:

Subject: I bumped into Father _____ at church
_____

Dear [Name],

Talk about coincidences. I bumped into Father _____ at church this past Sunday and learned that St. _____ is opening a new foster care division this coming March. One thing led to another, and he told me that Little Lamb Foster Care & Adoptive Services is in desperate need of social workers and foster/adoptive care counselors to fill several positions.

You might not recall my name, but hopefully I can help you to remember our meeting. I participated in an interview with you in early May of 2010 for the position of Foster Care Counselor with Little Lamb _____ facility.

We discussed my involvement with _____ Youth & Family Counseling Program at great length, and agreed I would be well suited for a similar position with Little Lamb as an Adoptive Care Counselor. Unfortunately, state and federal funding were reduced that month, leaving you with no other choice but to put a freeze on hiring.

As you can imagine, I am thrilled to learn of Little Lamb's new foster care program, and would welcome the opportunity to meet again to pick up where we left off. For your convenience, I am attaching my resume for your review. Thank you for your reconsideration. I look forward to speaking with you soon.

Sincerely,

(555) 555-1234

Old Boss—Networking

To:

From:

Cc:

Subject: Congratulations on the nomination!

Dear [Name],

Congratulations on your well-deserved nomination for the _____ Award. It speaks to the high degree of professional excellence for which you are known throughout our profession.

It's been a while since we've chatted, and I wanted to bring you up to date on what I've been doing. I joined a new company three years back, but unfortunately, the commute proved untenable, particularly during the winter months. I resigned—foolishly before I had secured my next gig, but four hours driving in the snow and ice every day was just too much. I was exhausted by the time I got to work.

This puts me back in the job market, and I wonder if you are aware of any HR positions that would capitalize on my ten-plus years' experience. Hopefully you will remember from when I reported to you that some of my strengths include:

- Excellent team-building and leadership skills

- Superb interpersonal skills and supervisory experience

- Developing and implementing human resource policies

- Recruiting and hiring a variety of hourly and salaried employees

- Extensive knowledge and experience in the healthcare arena

Feel free to pass my resume on to anyone who may have an appropriate opportunity, or give me a call if anyone comes to mind. Thank you in advance for your much-appreciated assistance. I shall vote and come to the awards dinner in the fall.

Sincerely,

(555) 555-1234

Old Friends Catch Up—Networking

To:

From:

Cc:

Subject: Good to catch up, muchacho!

Dear [Name],

It was good talking with you at last week's SHRM meeting, even more so to be remembered from "back in the day."

As mentioned, I recently got laid off in a merger and have re-entered the job market. Re the details you asked for: I have fifteen years' HR experience in employee benefit administration with a 700-unit clothing retailer.

I'm looking for opportunities in the retail world or any service-related organization. My experience includes pension plans and dental, life, and disability insurance. I have been responsible for all facets of management for the company's benefits plan, including accounting, maintenance, and liaison with both staff and negotiation with coverage providers.

For your information, my resume is attached. If any situations come to mind where you think my skills and background would fit or if you have any suggestions as to others with whom it might be beneficial for me to speak, it would be great to hear from you.

And good luck with the start of the school year. I don't envy you a thousand teenagers!

Sincerely,

[Your name]
[Your telephone number]

Professional Association—Networking

To:

From:

Cc:

Subject: Meet for coffee?

Hello [Name],

We spoke briefly at last week's Chamber of Commerce meeting, and I promised to follow up about the Construction Management job the city is seeking to fill.

With my background in construction, maintenance, and project management as well as operations and strategic leadership, I believe that I'm qualified and ready for this job. And what better job could there be than being part of ensuring that life in our city is the best it can be?

I have been highly successful at defining complex project plans, establishing budgets, outlining scope of work, and directly soliciting qualified contractors utilizing the bid process. I also offer extensive experience navigating through the paperwork and bureaucracy, forging productive alliances with key regulatory agencies to streamline permits and licenses for expedited project starts.

I appreciate you filling me in on the details of the project and have attached my resume as you suggested. I'd be excited to talk about the nuts and bolts of the job further. Could we meet for coffee one morning? You gave me your card, so I'll call your assistant to set something up.

Sincerely,

(555) 555-1234

Publishing, Networking

To:
From:
Cc:
Subject: Sincere thanks for the help ;-)
_____

Dear [Name],

It was a pleasure to meet with you for lunch today. I am grateful for the time you took out of your busy schedule to assist me in my job search.

It was fascinating to learn about the new technology that is changing the publishing field; we live in exciting times. I went straight to the bookstore to purchase the book that you recommended.

I will be contacting _____, as you suggested, and will let you know how things are progressing once I have met her.

Thanks again for your help. You will be hearing from me soon.

Yours sincerely,

(555) 555-1234

Thanks for the Referral—Got More?

To:

From:

Cc:

Subject: Thanks for the advice

Dear [Name],

Thanks for your advice yesterday. You gave me plenty to think about. I hope this letter finds you and your family well and that you are making good memories this holiday season.

I have been researching and making approaches to all three of the companies you recommended. Your suggestions were spot on and I have already had a reply from David Johannsen—having the name was immensely helpful, thanks.

Philippa, I genuinely appreciate the advice and assistance you have offered and if you get any more blinding flashes of genius please let me know; job hunting never gets any easier. Thank you, again, for all your help.

Sincerely,

(555) 555-1234
Attachment: resume

VP of Operations, Networking

To:
From:
Cc:
Subject: VP Operations
_____

Dear [Name],

_____ suggested I contact you after commenting that my background, business philosophy, and style reminded him of a CEO he had heard speak in Houston last year; apparently you were the hit of the conference.

I understand you too started on the shop floor. It has been several years since I took my first job as a machinist back in _____, __, but I have never lost my enthusiasm for finding more efficient and better ways of cutting costs while getting the job done. A machine shop is a great place to train critical thinking skills.

I worked my way up through the ranks from Foreman to Plant Supervisor to Manufacturing Engineer to Director of Operations and finally Vice President of Operations. Taking a swing at every new idea that came my way, I may have missed a few, but overall my batting average has been good. Three examples:

- Led a $340M manufacturing firm to earning ISO9002 certification on first attempt.
- Increased productivity at a plant in Mexico 34%, and reduced downtime 17%.
- Increased profits by 200% by restructuring production and delivery logistics.

I believe strongly in teams and am comfortable working with R&D, engineering, and marketing professionals. My colleagues have expressed appreciation for my direct and honest approach to people and problems.

Between jobs now, I am planning a fishing excursion on the Gulf. I will be arriving in _____ on ____ and would like to get together with you for lunch. I will give you a call the morning of the ____ to see if that can be arranged.

Please see my attached resume. I look forward to meeting you and exchanging ideas.

Sincerely,

(555) 555-1234

Web Development—Networking

To:
From:
Cc:
Subject: Web Development
_____

Hello, [Name],

Perhaps you remember our chance meeting at the Bio Asia-Pacific Conference
at the _____ on August 18 and 19, last month. In our brief conversation,
I shared with you the idea of utilizing Web Development as an administrative
tool. You expressed interest in the possibility of implementing such a system
within the _____ School of Medicine.

May I suggest a formal meeting to explore the idea?

I have some exciting and creative ideas, which may encourage you to take the
next step towards realizing the positive impact a content management system
would have within the School of Medicine. This would also be a great opportunity for us to discuss your goals and how an administrative Intranet would help
you reach them.

In addition, there has recently been spirited discussion within the IT community
on the topic of organizational continuity and its potential vulnerability due to
advances in technology.

If you recall, my background is in Web Planning and Development, with specific
skills in developing administrative Intranets and public websites, and designing
web-based software to address the internal and external reporting needs of
organizations.

Please see my attached resume attesting to my experience and specialties.
I will contact you within the next few days to discuss the possibility of meeting
with you.

Respectfully,

(555) 555-1234

LinkedIn.com
Networking Letters

LinkedIn is the leading social networking site for professionals. At LinkedIn, all communications to other members are sent through the site, so every letter has a similar format. As social networking sites exist for people to communicate and reach out to each other, you will notice that these letters, while polite and professional cut right to the chase.

If you know someone, or have known him or her in the past, you simply send a request to link. This will probably be fairly limited, so you will need to reach out to others that you don't know. The two easiest ways to do this are:

1. Send a request to link, through someone you know to the person you would like to know; the site automatically shows you the people who can provide the patch for your introduction.
2. You can join special-interest groups; there are hundreds, maybe thousands. Then as a member of a group, you can approach any other member directly for a link, based on your mutual membership of that group.

Here are a few examples of networking letters to and from members of the LinkedIn.com social networking site.

LinkedIn: Networking Letter #1

This was sent to a member of a common interest group.

_____ _____ has sent you a message.

Date: **/**/2010

Subject: Exchange leads?

Hello _____,

I came across your profile on LinkedIn while doing a job search here on LI. We're both part of the SharePoint Experts Group, and I thought it might make sense that we're connected. Let me know if I can be of assistance in your networking efforts here on LI. Perhaps we could talk and exchange leads?

Sincerely,

Your Name
(555) 555-1234
you@email.com

LinkedIn: Networking Letter #2

LinkedIn lets you contact those you've known previously.
Here's a letter reconnecting with a past coworker.

_____ _____ has sent you a message.

Date: **/**/2010

Subject: Blast from the past

_____,

I just came across your profile, and thought I'd reach out. We both worked at _____ in the late '90s, and I believe I may have hired you. I'd like to add you to my network, catch up, and see how we might help each other.

Sincerely,

Your Name
(555) 555-1234
you@email.com

LinkedIn: Introduction Request #1

You can use LinkedIn to get introductions to people you don't know through people you *do* know. Here is a networking letter asking a networking contact at LinkedIn for an introduction to a prominent headhunter, a member of their network. This follows the sequence of emails through to its conclusion: Someone looking for a job locates a recruiter with an open requisition.

To:

Hi Martin,
I hope that things are well. I see you know Olga Ocon; she recruits for jobs in my profession, so I was wondering if you could introduce me to her. Please could you pass on my request?
Thank you,

To: _____ _____

From **Martin Yate**

Hi Olga,

I know a talented software guy, Jack Krainski, who is interested in connecting with you. His communication to me is below. May you have fruitful conversations.

Best,

From _____ _____

To: Martin Yate

Date: July 28, 2010. 6.18PM

Martin,
Yes, have Jack send me an invite. In fact, he can email me directly if LI is letting us mention email addresses this week ;-). If he is the one I just checked out, I think I have a position that he would be interested in—the job that is local to DFW. This could be ideal timing.

LinkedIn: Introduction Request #2

This letter asks a networking contact at LinkedIn for an introduction to a member of their network.

_____ _____ has sent you a message.

Date: **/**/2017

Subject: NBI Certified

Hi,
I am asking for an introduction to Clarice Rubenstein so that I can pursue a job opportunity with one of her clients. Thanks for taking the time to make this introduction for me.
Sincerely,

LinkedIn: Introduction Request #1

This letter includes an introduction request and a note to the target contact.

Subject: Your advice is working!

Hello Martin,

I am beginning to get some hits and interview requests since I began using your *Knock 'em Dead* books a couple of weeks ago. The American Red Cross is the place I would most like to end up and I am trying to get past the cyber wall barrier without much luck. You know Bob Chen who might be able to help; would you be kind enough to pass my introduction request along? It's below the signature. Thanks for all of your help.

(Your name)

Hello Bob,

I am currently interested in a recovery planning job at Red Cross with the Field Operations Group. It's a job I'm doing with CDC now, but I am having trouble getting any personal contact with the hiring decision-makers.
Do you have any insight on how the process works or how I might be able to reach out on a personal level to the recruiting department? Thanks for any info you may have.

Sincerely,

Your Name
(555) 555-1234

LinkedIn: Introduction Request #2

Here's another example of a request for an introduction along with a contact note.

Subject: Thank you for inviting me into your network

Hi _____ _____,

Thank you for accepting me into your network, Martin! Please let me know if you are comfortable with forwarding my request for the introduction to John Rogers that follows my signature. Please let me know of anything I can do in return.

Thank you,

Your Name

Hello _____ _____,

I am a seasoned Operations and Project Management specialist with a proven track record in optimizing operations to achieve maximum production and profit potential.
Please take a moment to review my profile, and let me know if you are interested in an exploratory conversation. I am of course happy to send my resume if you can send me your email address.

I look forward to your response.

Regards,

Your Name

LinkedIn: Direct Approach

You get ten free inmails a month. This allows you to directly approach people you don't know and can't get an introduction to otherwise. Note the use of good background information.

Subject: Risk mitigation–related question

Dear Jacqueline,

I was very impressed with what I learned about your new program at the Export-Import Bank Conference last week. Risk mitigation is my wheelhouse.

I am working on my dissertation and I would like to come up to explore your ground-breaking initiatives further. Would this be possible? I look forward to hearing from you soon.

Best,

LinkedIn: Connect to Executive

LinkedIn allows you to connect on many levels of the target organization. Here's a networking letter to connect with an executive at a vendor with whose product the sender is certified.

Subject: NBI Certified

Hello _____,

I'm one of NBI's authorized Partners, and would like to add you to my contacts here on LinkedIn. _____ _____ or _____ _____ can verify my affiliation.

Sincerely,

Your Name

LinkedIn: Letter to a Recruiter

Subject: Recruiter seeks advice

Dear _____

Elderly parents are bringing me back home to Philly. I'm a senior-level staffing and recruitment professional who is seeking opportunity in the greater Philadelphia area.
I am talking with a few companies right now, and as you are a leading corporate recruiter I'd appreciate your insight into the local market and players. In this respect, I'm hoping we might connect and chat, is this possible?

Sincerely,

Your Name

RESURRECTION LETTERS

Analyst—Resurrection

To:

From:

Cc:

Subject: Lost analyst?

Dear [Name],

I must have been one of the first people you spoke with about the Analyst job posting, because at the time you seemed very interested, as was I. However, when I called back you had received so many calls for the position you didn't know one from the other. That's understandable, so I hope I can stir your memory and, more importantly, your interest.

I have a solid programming and project development background and have worked in web applications for seven years now, with a special focus on e-commerce for the last three years. What's even better is my hobby: my work—we talked about both building kit computers back in the day.

I have attached a resume for your perusal. But in case you don't want to read all the details, here it is in short:

- I have seven years developing websites
- I have three years in e-commerce
- I have two years in e-commerce/affiliate integration
- I have two years working extensively on cloud-based applications

I look forward to speaking with you again, so please don't hesitate to call me at (555) 555-1234, or hit me with an email.

Sincerely,

Attachment: resume

Headhunter Resurrection

To:

From:

Cc:

Subject: Your Pipeline Management searches

Dear [Name],

    I am in the pipeline management field with considerable experience and achievements. I am looking for a management position that leverages the experience and abilities reflected in the attached resume. I am open to relocating in the United States and overseas.
I sent my resume awhile back but recognize that these things sometimes get mislaid. If any positions become available, I would be happy to discuss the details. Thanks for your consideration.

Sincerely,

(555) 555-1234
Attachment: resume

Job Fair Resurrection

To:

From:

Cc:

Subject: Thanks for the advice

Dear [Name],

Firstly, I want to thank you for the time you spent with me on August 4 at the Detroit Convention Center job fair. You passed me on to an assistant to collect my resume and phone number.

In the short time we talked I shared my qualifications and interest in the QA positions you are trying to fill—I not only have the experience you require, it is with one of your direct competitors.

With that in mind, I have attached my resume for your review. To summarize:

- I have an extensive history of working in QA in technology manufacturing.
- I am a reliable and committed professional—we are both members of the local chapter of the Quality Assurance Association.
- I have current experience in exactly the same area of specialization.

This resume is only a hint of who I am—words on paper cannot replace a personal conversation. Therefore, would you please consider my request for a face-to-face interview so that you may evaluate my qualifications, abilities, drive, and enthusiasm for yourself?

Yours is a job I can nail, yours is a job for which I am supremely qualified, yours is a company I have always wanted to join. Would you take a look at the attached resume and then give me a call or an email to arrange a meeting?
Thank you for your consideration, and I look forward to meeting with you again soon.

Sincerely,

(555) 555-1234
Attachment: resume

Keep Me in Mind

To:

From:

Cc:

Subject: Director of HR selection

Dear [Name],

Congratulations on the selection of your new Director of Human Resources! I hope this new person meets and exceeds your expectations.

I appreciated the chance to apply for the position and am grateful for the consideration you have given me throughout this process. Although I am obviously disappointed at not being the successful candidate, I remain interested in potential opportunities with your organization.

If for any reason or at any time this position opens up again, please be aware that I will be interested.

I know my seven years' experience in HR plus my organization, communication skills, and flexibility would make me an asset. Thank you for all your time and consideration. I look forward to speaking with you again.

Sincerely,

[Telephone #]

Line Lift Driver—Resurrection

To:

From:

Cc:

Subject: Remember the snowstorm on Dec 23rd?

Dear [Name],

We met for an interview on December 23 in the middle of that major snowstorm, regarding opportunities for Lift Line Operators. Since then I have obtained a CDL-B Learner's Permit with Passenger and Air-Brake endorsements.

The holidays have come and gone, and because of the weather and time of year when we met, I thought I should follow up with you.

I am writing to reiterate my sincere interest in a Lift Line Driver position and hope to speak with you soon to arrange a further interview. I look forward to talking with you soon.

Sincerely,

(555) 555-1234
Attachment: resume

Lost in the Shuffle

To:

From:

Cc:

Subject: Lost in the shuffle?

Dear [Name],

I must have been one of the first people you spoke with about the Programmer job posting, because at the time you seemed very interested, as was I. However, when I called back you had received so many calls for the position you didn't know one from the other. That's understandable, so I hope I can stir your memory and, more importantly, your interest.

I have a solid programming and project development background in both the Windows and Macintosh worlds, and have worked in web applications for five years now. What's even better is my hobby: my work.

You had some ideas for children's software and thought having kids would help when working on such software. You had asked if I had children and I do: a four-and-a-half-year-old daughter and a four-and-a-half-month-old daughter.

My oldest uses _____ on my Macintosh at home and double-clicks away without any assistance from my wife or myself. She has learned a great deal from "playing" with it and is already more computer literate than I ever expected. We need more software like _____ to help stir the minds of our kids.

I have attached a resume for your perusal. But in case you don't want to read all the details, here it is in short:

- I have 6 years' programming and development experience in Windows.
- I have 3 years' programming and development experience on the Macintosh.
- I am currently the Senior Developer for Macintosh programming here at _____ Corp.
- I have 2 years' experience working extensively on cloud-based applications.

I look forward to speaking with you again, so please don't hesitate to call me, (555) 555-1234, or hit me with an email.

Sincerely,

(555) 555-1234

Network Contact

To:

From:

Cc:

Subject: Father O'Rourke says hello ;-)

_____

Dear [Name],

I'm not sure if you will remember me, but hopefully I can help you to remember our meeting. I participated in an interview with you in early May of 2015 for a position as a Foster Care Counselor with the Little Lambs facility. We had two very positive interviews but funding was reduced that month leaving you with no other choice but to put a freeze on hiring.

Anyway, I bumped into Father O'Rourke last week and learned that the city is opening a new foster-care operation in the next few months and that you are heading up the initiative. One word led to another, and he told me that they are in desperate need of social workers and foster/adoptive care counselors. He mentioned your name; I recalled our meeting, and he suggested I reach out to you and pass on his best regards.

We discussed my involvement with the church Youth & Family Counseling Program at great length and agreed I would be well suited for a similar position as an Adoptive Care Counselor with the new program you are leading.

I would welcome the opportunity to meet again to pick up where we left off. For your convenience, I am attaching my resume for your review. Thank you for your reconsideration. I look forward to speaking with you soon.

Sincerely,

Attachment: resume

New Hiring Budgets Opening Up

To:
From:
Cc:
Subject: SOX 404 and COSO Frameworks

Dear [Name],

We spoke a couple of months back, before the new audit hiring budget had opened up and, as you suggested we keep in touch, I'm reaching out to take the temperature on your audit needs.

As a memory jogger, I am the internal audit and operational risk management woman with extensive experience in highly matrixed shared services in the technology sector. I'm also the go-to person for SOX 404 testing and internal controls evaluation with the COSO Framework. My strengths include:

Evaluate Internal Controls using the COSO Framework
Identify internal control deficiencies
Perform SOX 404 Testing

My attached resume should demonstrate that these credentials derived from highly matrixed technology companies qualify me as a good match for your audit and operational risk management needs. I would enjoy reconnecting and the opportunity to learn how I might add further depth and reliability to your team. I'm at (555) 555-1234 and look forward to the conversation.

Sincerely,

(555) 555-1234

New Skills

To:
From:
Cc:
Subject: Remember the snowstorm on Dec 23rd?

Dear [Name],

We met on _____ site on December 23 in the middle of that major snowstorm, and spoke regarding opportunities for Lift Line Operators. Since then I have obtained a **CDL-B Learner's Permit with Passenger and Air-Brake endorsements**.

I am writing to reiterate my sincere interest in a **Lift Line Driver** position, and hope to speak with you soon to learn what my next steps would be in order to further my candidacy. I look forward to talking with you soon.

Sincerely,

(555) 555-1234

Operations Manager—Resurrection

To:

From:

Cc:

Subject: You were so right!

Dear [Name],

Four months ago you and I discussed an Operations Management job in your Northfield facility, and you arranged further meetings with management in that facility. I was well along in my job search and shortly thereafter, as you know, I accepted a position with _____.

You warned me about the issues there, but I had to learn the hard way that all that glitters is not gold. You were absolutely right that I would have difficulties in that environment. I should have been more patient, but as a family man, after that layoff I had obligations.

I would like to reopen our discussions if a similar position is available, or if not, then when one opens up please put me first on your list. I've attached my resume and hope we can get together. I'll call to catch up in the next couple of days.

Sincerely,

(555) 555-1234
Attachment: resume

Resurrection

To:

From:

Cc:

Subject: Impressive meeting!

Dear [Name],

Thank you for the interview we had last week for the Community Team Director position. I genuinely appreciated the chance to discuss your vision for the CET program.

Although another candidate was ultimately selected for this important position, I was pleased to be among the short list of applicants under consideration.

I believe that my nine years' experience with the City of _____ provide me with a wealth of knowledge and expertise that can be beneficial to the city, perhaps when a similar position becomes available.

Additionally, I'd like to offer myself as a candidate for other roles where you feel my capabilities can further the objectives of the city. Please keep me in mind if other opportunities should arise where my talents would be an asset.

I look forward to hearing from you.

Sincerely,

(555) 555-1234

ACCEPTANCE LETTERS

Acceptance: Fast Start

From:

To

Cc:

Subject: Marcom Manager job offer

Dear [Name],

Thank you for the job offer for the Marketing Communications Manager position. I am delighted to accept your offer of employment and look forward to a fast start with the projects we discussed during the selection process; we agree that the sales forecasting and strategic market planning for the core product line is top priority.

I am honored that you chose me to lead your marketing communications efforts. I am fully confident in delivering the results we discussed.

Per your instructions, I will contact the Human Resources department on Monday morning to arrange an orientation appointment. I look forward to meeting with you to start putting together a plan of attack; maybe at lunch after my orientation appointment?

Sincerely,

(555) 555-1234

Delayed Start

To:
From:
Cc:
Subject: Reference _____ job offer _____

Dear [Name],

I would like to express my appreciation for your letter offering me the position of _____
_____ in your Department at a starting salary of $__, ___ per year.

I was very impressed with the team and facilities in _____, and am writing to confirm my
acceptance of your offer. If it is acceptable to you, I will report to work on Date. I need to offer
proper notice, and then wish to take two weeks to go see my parents in Chennai. I do hope this
is acceptable.

Let me once again express my appreciation for your offer and my excitement about joining your
_____ staff. I look forward to my association with _____, and know my contributions
will be in line with your expectations.

Sincerely,

(555) 555-1234

Happy to Accept Job Offer

To:

From:

Cc:

Subject: Happy to accept the job offer and join the team

Dear [Name],

I want to thank you for the privilege of joining your staff as _____ _____. Your flexibility and cooperation in the counter-negotiations were much appreciated. Thank you for making every effort to make the pending transition a smooth one.

Per your request, I am providing this letter, for my official file.

"In that your organization is a competitor of my previous employer, and in that this organization seeks to maintain goodwill and high levels of integrity within the industry, it should be duly noted that neither you nor any representative of your organization sought me as a prospective employee. It was my identification of a possible position, and solely my pursuits toward your company, that resulted in my resignation as Senior Director to join your firm as Managing Consultant."

If I can provide additional clarification on this matter, or assist in protecting the ethics of your company, notify me at your convenience. I look forward to starting with your team on the _____ of _____.

Sincerely,

(555) 555-1234

No Piracy Agreement

To:

From:

Cc:

Subject: Start dates

Dear [Name],

I want to thank you for the opportunity to join your team as _____ . Your flexibility and cooperation in our negotiations are much appreciated. Thank you for making every effort to make the pending transition a smooth one for me and my family.

Per your request, I am providing this letter, for my official file.

"In that your organization is a competitor of my previous employer, and in that this organization seeks to maintain goodwill and high levels of integrity within the industry, it should be duly noted that neither you, nor any representative of your organization, sought me as a prospective employee. It was my identification of a possible position, and solely my pursuits toward your company, that resulted in my resignation as Senior Director, to join your firm as Managing Consultant."

I look forward to starting with your team on the 27th of October.

Sincerely,

(555) 555-1234

R&D Acceptance

To:

From:

Cc:

Subject: VP R&D Acceptance

Dear [Name],

I understand and accept the conditions of employment that you explained in the offer letter. Please accept my formal acceptance of your offer to join your firm as Vice President of R&D.

I will contact your personnel department this week to request any paperwork I might complete for their records prior to my starting date. Also, I will schedule a physical examination for insurance purposes. I would appreciate your forwarding any reading material you feel might hasten my initiation.

Yesterday I tendered my resignation and worked out a mutually acceptable notice time of four weeks, which should allow me ample time to finalize my business and personal affairs here and be ready for work on schedule for our agreed-upon date, six weeks from today on Monday, March 22nd.

I anxiously anticipate joining the team and look forward to many new challenges. You, your board, and your staff have been most professional and helpful throughout this hiring process. Thank you for your confidence and support.

Sincerely,

(555) 555-1234

NEGOTIATION LETTERS

Bump Up the Money, Please

To:
From:
Cc:
Subject: Operations Management questions

Dear [Name],

I want to thank you for your invitation to join the company. I have reviewed the offer of position and compensation, as presented in your letter dated _____, 2017. I know my skills will be supportive of the existing leadership and that my thorough competency and good judgment will enable senior management to focus on new aspects of business development and achieve corporate goals and objectives that will be beneficial to us all.

I would like to ask for clarification on a few items prior to providing you with a formal acceptance. I believe this will enable both parties to begin the partnership more informed of mutual goals and expectations.

Per the breakdown provided:

- I accept the 401(K) plan as proposed
- I accept the paid holiday and personal days plan as proposed
- I accept the Direct Payroll Deposit plan as proposed (if elected)
- I accept the Medical, Dental, Vision, Pharmacy, and Life Insurance benefits as proposed, contingent on factors clarified below

Points of clarification:

- What is available in regard to "Stock Options"?
- What are the "standard hours of operation" for ABC employees?
- Would it be possible to have a "Performance Evaluation" at six months?

Finally, in light of the "out-of-pocket expenses" correspondent to the medical benefits, how might we agree to get the annual base salary to $__,___? I am open to a number of different options to achieve this goal, including profit sharing, commission, or 5% annual bonus arrangement.

I am excited about the long-term possibilities that joining your team offers. Again, I want to thank you for the gracious offer. I look forward to finalizing these minor details very soon.

Sincerely,

[Your name]
[Your telephone number]

A Commission Issue

To:

From:

Cc:

Subject: Regarding the _____ job offer
_____

Dear [Name],

I have reviewed your letter and the specific breakdown regarding compensation. I believe there to be a few items to clarify, prior to providing you with a formal acceptance. I do not consider any of the items to be "deal breakers" in any way. I also do not perceive them to be issues that cannot be discussed, as we are, in fact, moving ahead.

The primary concern has to do with the commission structure, as opposed to salary plus commission, to which I have grown accustomed. From a practical perspective I need to have some financial coverage for the start-up period: the time it will take me to make sales, collect the money, and the lead time this takes to go through the accounting and payroll system. I also need this because I will be shifting from a biweekly salary schedule to a monthly format.

I am hoping that as per the industry norm, you will absorb some of this start-up cost. I am therefore asking for straight salary for the first two weeks and then a draw against commission up to the end of the 90-day probationary period.

The second clarification revolves around the 401(k) program; the percentages, timeframes, and terms. This is something we can discuss over the course of the next two weeks. You may even be able to pass something specific on to me in writing.

With these two concerns articulated, I want you to know that I will be meeting with the owner of our company tomorrow morning to discuss my plans for departure. In fairness to him and to my current client load, I could not start full-time with you for 21 days.

I would like to set a time for us to have dinner one evening next week, so you can meet my wife and we can talk a bit less formally.

Looking forward to what lies ahead.

Sincerely,

(555) 555-1234

The Devil's in the Details

To:

From:

Cc:

Subject: Executive Administration job offer

Dear [Name],

I am excited by the invitation to join the company as an Executive Administrator for the CMO. However, before I give you my formal acceptance there are a handful of items on which I need clarification:

- Detailed description of insurance benefits.
- Realistic analysis of the corporate stock and 401(K) plans.
- Written explanation of educational reimbursement allowance.
- The mobility plan seems very reasonable, but I would like specifics on the Permanent Work aspect.
- Relocation coverage: is it an allowance or reimbursement of actual expenses incurred in the move? What are my tax obligations, and does the company cover them?
- Detailed explanation of the Variable Pay Plan.

I hope to be able to tender my resignation and give you a formal start date as soon as I have a clear understanding on these issues.

Respectfully Yours,

(555) 555-1234

Low-Ball Salary

To:

From:

Cc:

Subject: Forensic Accountant Offer

Dear [Name],

I am excited by the invitation to join the company as a Forensic Accountant. The position and responsibilities are consistent with my career goals, and I am genuinely excited about the opportunity.

There is, however, one issue we need to address: In our conversations, I communicated to you that I was making $__K while working part-time and going to school. The salary offer subsequently made by the company is substantially lower and represents a pay cut.

This dollar amount will simply not make it feasible for me to meet my financial obligations. I am really interested in the job, but anything less than $___K salary will make my decision very difficult.
I hope we can discuss these issues in the very near future and trust that we will soon be working together.

Respectfully Yours,

(555) 555-1234

Salary Beneath Industry Norm

To:

From:

Cc:

Subject: Data Center Specialist job offer

Dear [Name],

Thank you for the job offer. Your state-of-the-art data center with those mammoth Samsung servers would afford me the opportunity to make a contribution while continuing to grow professionally in an ever-evolving industry. The job promises challenge and a high level of professional commitment that I am more than willing to deliver.

It is my understanding that as the Data Center Specialist, my communication skills with technology and nontechnology management will be critical to performance success. With my experience in troubleshooting technical problems, I know that technology only becomes truly useful when it can be translated into user effectiveness. My expertise integrates both of these critical components that are key in the job and by this time I am sure my references have already confirmed this with you.

However, the salary range for this type of position in our industry normally falls between \$__,_____ and \$__,___. I would like to request that we reconsider the starting offer of \$__,___. Of course, I appreciate the generous benefits package that you provide and take this into account as I hope we can give the starting salary a bump to bring the package in line with industry norms.

I look forward to hearing from you and hope that we can reach an agreement that will enable me to begin my career with you on June 4.

Sincerely,

(555) 555-1234

Salary Negotiation

To:
From:
Cc:
Subject: Regarding the Territory Manager job offer

Dear [Name],

Thank you for the job offer and especially the breakdown regarding compensation. There are a few items I need to to clarify before giving you my formal acceptance. None of these items are "deal breakers" in any way.

My primary concern has to do with the commission structure, as opposed to salary plus commission, to which I have always been accustomed. From a practical perspective I need to have some financial coverage for the start-up period: It will take me some time to make sales and collect the money, as well as the time this takes to go through the accounting and payroll systems. I also need this because I will be shifting from a biweekly salary schedule to a monthly format.
I am hoping that, as per the industry norm, you will absorb some of this start-up cost. I would appreciate a straight salary for the first two weeks and then a draw against commission up to the end of the ninety-day probationary period.

The second clarification revolves around the 401(K) program; the percentages, time frames, and terms. This is something we can discuss over the course of the next two weeks. You may even be able to pass something specific on to me in writing.

If you feel we can come to accommodation on these issues I will be able to start three weeks from the date of my formal resignation, which I hope to have resolved within the next couple of days.

Looking forward to what lies ahead,

Sincerely,

(555) 555-1234

Rejection Letters

Department Manager—Rejection

To:

From:

Cc:

Subject: Department Manager opening

Dear [Name],

I would like to take this opportunity to thank you for the interview last week, and while I very much appreciate your offer for the position of Department Manager, I feel that I must regretfully decline. Having worked in management for seven years, I am confident that my skills will be best applied in a position with more responsibility and bottom-line accountability.

As we discussed, I very much look forward to talking again in January about how I might contribute to the company in the capacity of Unit Manager—now that is a job I can sink my teeth into! Roll on the New Year!

Sincere regards,

(555) 555-1234

Executive Assistant—Rejection

To:

From:

Cc:

Subject: ref: EA job offer

Dear [Name],

It was a pleasure meeting with you to discuss your needs for an executive assistant. Our time together was energizing and informative.

As we discussed during our meetings, the primary purpose of interviews is to assess the fit between the individual and the position and to explore areas of mutual interest. I was well along in my job search when we spoke and intimated I was close to receiving offers.

As I have accepted a position that is well suited to my qualifications and experience, I must withdraw myself from consideration. Thank you for interviewing me and giving me the opportunity to learn more about your operation. You have a fine team, and I would have enjoyed working with you; perhaps another opportunity will arise in our future.

Best wishes to you and your staff, and I look forward to running into you again one of these days.

Sincerely,

(555) 555-1234

Not This Job, Maybe Something Bigger

To:
From:
Cc:
Subject: Appreciate your interest

Dear [Name],

Thank you for your email updating me on the status of the telecommunications project we discussed in our recent telephone conversation.

Although I genuinely appreciate your consideration for the Team Supervisor position, at this time I feel my best interests are to pursue a position more closely aligned with my level of experience, achievements, and demonstrated managerial skills.

I remain most interested in opportunities with your company, and would ask that you keep my name in consideration for other positions that would more fully capitalize on my knowledge and expertise. Thank you for your time and interest.

Sincerely,

(555) 555-1234

Policy Manager—Rejection

To:

From:

Cc:

Subject: Policy Manager job offer

Dear [Name],

I would like to thank you for offering me the position of Policy Manager. I am extremely grateful for the opportunity and time I had to meet you, Lewis, Jamie, Jane, Connie, and Robert over the last few weeks and appreciate the time you gave in considering me for a position in your organization.

It was quite a challenging decision for me, as I was genuinely impressed by the well-deserved reputation of your company—especially the CRM group that I would be involved with. Everything reinforced the great experience I had working at your Santa Clara site as a temporary employee.

However, I have made a decision to accept an offer that is better aligned with my immediate career goals. I wish you and the CRM group much continued success. I sincerely hope that we stay in touch and that our professional paths cross again. Thank you again for your time and consideration.

Sincerely,

(555) 555-1234

Telecommunications Analyst—Rejection

To:

From:

Cc:

Subject: RE: Telecommunications Analyst discussions

Dear [Name],

Thank you for your email updating me on the status of the telecommunications project we discussed in our recent telephone conversation.

Although I genuinely appreciate your consideration for the Team Supervisor position, I feel my best interests at this time are to pursue a position more closely aligned with my level of experience, achievements, and managerial skills.

I enjoyed our meetings on both a professional and personal level and remain most interested in opportunities with your company. I would ask that you keep my name in consideration for other positions that would more fully capitalize on my knowledge and expertise. Thank you for your time and interest.

Sincerely,

(555) 555-1234

VP Marketing—Rejection

From:

To:

Cc:

Subject: Declining job offer

Dear [Name],

I appreciated meeting with the Board and the Search Committee to discuss the position of V.P. Marketing. I was very favorably impressed with the organization and believe that if selected, my contributions would have more than justified your judgment.

However, I would ask that my name be withdrawn from further consideration. I have recently been offered a challenging and rewarding opportunity that is perfect for my career at this time. The time frames involved in this transition (you know I have been laid off and my last day is Friday) have made it necessary for me to make a decision without delay, and I have chosen to accept this offer.

I remain enormously impressed with what you are doing on the international stage and would be most interested in keeping touch. Perhaps the future may present another opportunity for us to talk. I wish you the best of luck in this current search. Thank you, again, for your time and consideration.

Sincerely,

(555) 555-1234

RESIGNATION LETTERS

You will notice that all these resignation letter examples are laid out as traditional letters rather than emails. This is because an email resignation is entirely inappropriate and unprofessional. Properly done resignations are made in person. As we noted earlier, by far the easiest way to handle this awkward situation is to:

1. Ask for a meeting.
2. Have the letter typed and in an envelope.

Walk in, sit down, offer the letter, and let your manager read it. When it is worded as these samples are, the ensuing conversation should be smooth and focused on the transition.

John Singh
Director Logistics

[Date]

Dear [Name],

Please accept my resignation as ___[title]_____. I have accepted a position as ____[title]_____ in Ohio. I intend to make this change as painless as possible for someone who has always supported me. We can discuss a mutually acceptable termination date and what has to be achieved by that date after you have read this letter.

My reports are readily able to handle operations until you find a suitable replacement; you could do worse than look at Angela Ciccine as an interim leader and may find that she is well qualified to take over my responsibilities on a permanent basis.

My decision to leave was made after long and careful consideration of all factors affecting the company, my family, and my career. Although I regret leaving many friends here, I feel that the change will be beneficial to all parties.

Finally, I can only express my sincere appreciation to you and the entire board for all your support, cooperation, and encouragement over the years. I will always remember my stay at_____ for the personal growth it afforded and for the numerous friendships made.

I hope our parting can be without acrimony and most importantly that you and I stay in touch.

Yours truly,

(555) 555-1234

MIS Resignation from First Job

To: John Smith
        Business Analyst
        Very Important Company
From:
Cc:
Subject: Resignation notification

Dear Mr. Smith,

This letter is to notify you that I am resigning my position with _____
effective _____.
In order to achieve the career goals that I've set for myself, I have accepted a
higher-level Systems Operator position with another company. This position will
give me an opportunity to become more involved in the technical aspects of
setting up networking systems.

I have enjoyed my work here very much and want to thank you and the rest of the
MIS Department for all the encouragement and support you have always given
me.
Please know that I am available to help with any staff training or offer assistance
in any way that will make my departure as easy as possible for the department.

I want to wish everyone the best of luck in the future. Thanks again for giving me
my start in a profession I love. I will always hold you in the highest esteem,
_____.

Sinccrely,

[Your name]

CARLA GOMEZ

[Date]

Dear [Name]:

Please accept this letter as written confirmation of my resignation as a per diem on-call CCU nurse with _____ Hospital. My permanent part-time employment was scheduled to begin April 7th. However, in the interim, I accepted a permanent full-time position with another healthcare organization.

Joining your staff on a full-time basis would have been my dream, but full-time work is a necessity so I needed to take this opportunity. I hope that one day in the future I might have the opportunity to work for you again in a permanent full-time capacity. Until then, thank you for the opportunity to be a part of your team.

Sincerely,

Carla Gomez

Requested Resignation

To: The Other Place
        Shirley Jones, R.N.
        Sad Sisters of Mercy Hospital
From:
Cc:
Subject: Requested resignation

Dear Ms. Jones,

As requested by _____, Nursing Manager, I am submitting this letter as written confirmation of my resignation as a per diem on-call CCU nurse with _____ Hospital. My permanent part-time employment was scheduled to begin April 7th. However, in the interim, I accepted a permanent full-time position with _____Hospital.

On April 3rd I met with _____, Human Resources Administrator, to inform her of my decision. I expressed a desire to honor my commitment with the understanding that the need for flexibility in my schedule would be taken into consideration. _____ contacted _____ to discuss an alternative employment arrangement. Subsequently, my status from permanent part-time was changed to per diem on call.

Immediately upon completion of the mandatory two-week orientation period, I was faced with a schedule conflict. As a result of an apparent miscommunication, I was scheduled to do my floor orientation from April 21st through 25th. I approached _____, Nursing Manager, to resolve the conflict, and learned that she was completely unaware of both my situation and agreement between _____, Human Resources, and myself. As a result, my resignation seemed to be the logical solution.

_____, it was never my intention to cause problems within your administration; therefore, please accept my apology for any inconvenience experienced. Thank you for the opportunity to be a part of your staff.

Sincerely,

[Your name]
[Your telephone number]

Resignation after 10 Years and a Good Relationship

To:
From:
Cc:
Subject: A new beginning

Dear [Name],

As we discussed this morning, I am writing to confirm my resignation as _____ from _____. Beginning on _____, I will start a new position with ____ as a _____.

The last ten years with _____ have been a time of personal fulfillment and enormous professional growth for me, and I so appreciate all that you've done to mentor my development and create such a strong sense of team spirit and such an energizing workplace.

I am proud of the contributions I've made under your guidance, but the time has come for me to take a new direction. This decision was by no means an easy one, but I am confident that this new challenge represents a positive step toward fulfilling my long-term career objectives.

Thanks again for all of your support. I wish you and the company all the best for the future. I shall remember my colleagues and the company with great fondness and respect.

Sincerely,

[Your name]
[Your telephone number]

Dustin Chen

Baton Rouge, LA 70518

(504) 495-0538
Dustin.Chen@mountain.com

Date

Name of Person
Title
Name of Company
Address

Dear [Name]:

Please accept my resignation of my position as Sales Representative for the metropolitan area, effective January 25. I am offering two weeks' notice so that my territory can be effectively serviced during the transition, with the least amount of inconvenience to our clients.

I thank you for the sales training and have enjoyed very much working under your leadership. It is largely due to the excellent experience I gained working on your team that I am now able to pursue this growth opportunity in Training and Development.

During the next two weeks, I am willing to help in every way to make the transition as smooth as possible. This includes assisting in recruiting and training my replacement. If I can be of assistance to you or my replacement after this time, perhaps in giving insights on particular clients, I am more than happy to do so. Please let me know if there is anything specific that you would like me to do.

Again, it has been a true honor working as a part of your group. I shall remember the team and especially your leadership and guidance with fondness for many years. I hope we stay in touch.

Sincerely,

Benke Berjemo

3487 Avenue C, Lakewood, Ohio 44107
(330) 278-8976
b.berjemo@Reamemcovertraxx.com

January 4, 2017

Dear [Name]:

This letter is to notify you that I am resigning my position with the company, with two weeks notice; my last day will be _____.

I have enjoyed my work here very much and want to thank you for the encouragement and support you have always given me. Please know that I am available to help with staff training or in any other way that will make my departure as trouble-free as possible for our operations.

I have accepted a higher-level Systems Operator position with another company that will give me an opportunity to become more involved in the technical aspects of setting up networking systems.

Thanks for giving me my start in a profession I love. I will always hold you in the highest esteem.

Sincerely,
BB

THANK YOU LETTERS

I Landed a Job and You Helped

To:
From:
Cc:
Subject: I landed a job and you helped, thanks Jack

Dear [Name],

I want you to be among the first to know that my job search has come to a very successful conclusion. I have accepted the position of _____ at _____, Inc., located in _____.

I appreciate all the help and support you have provided over the last several months. It has made this awful job search process much easier for me. I look forward to staying in contact with you. Please let me know when I can be of any assistance to you in the future. Thank you.

Sincerely,

(555) 555-1234
Your Initials

Senior Admin—Thank You

To:
From:
Cc:
Subject: I finally did it!

Dear [Name],

I am happy to tell you that I received and accepted an offer of employment just after Thanksgiving. I am now employed by _____ as a _____.

My duties include responsibility for all _____ software (General Ledger, Accounts Payable, Accounts Receivable, and Fixed Assets) for worldwide plus the first-year training of several entry-level employees. I am enjoying my new responsibility and being fully employed again.

I want to thank you not only for all your help the past several months during my search for employment but also for your understanding and friendly words of encouragement. It really meant something in some dark hours. Thanks, muchacho.

If there is ever anything I can do for you please call me. I hope you and your family have a wonderful holiday season, and much luck and happiness in the New Year.

Most sincerely,

[Your name]
[Your telephone number]

Thank You

From:

To:

Cc:

Subject: Thanks for the help, Janice

Dear Janice,

I want you to be among the first to know that the living hell of my job search has come to an end. I have accepted the position of _____ at _____, Inc., located in _____.

I really appreciate the leads and emotional support you've given me over the last few months. It really made the awful job search process much easier for me. Please let me know when I can be of any assistance to you in the future. Let's stay in touch. Thank you.

Sincerely,

(555) 555-1234

Thank You

From:

To:

Cc:

Subject: You were right, I finally did it!

Dear [Name],

I am happy to tell you that I received and accepted an offer of employment just after Labor Day, and I started at _____, as a _____.

My duties include responsibility of all _____ software (General Ledger, Accounts Payable, Accounts Receivable, and Fixed Assets) for worldwide plus the first-year training of several entry-level employees. I am enjoying my new responsibilities and am happy to be gainfully employed again. A word of advice about surviving a layoff: If ever you hear rumors of cutbacks, believe them. I got caught in a 750-person downsizing, and in my town getting that many people absorbed into other companies caused misery for many of us . . . and all because I believed HR when they told me "no layoffs" three months prior.

Thanks for all your help in my search for employment and also for your understanding and friendly words of encouragement. It really meant something in the dark hours; thanks, muchacho.

If there is ever anything I can do for you please call me. I hope you and your family have a wonderful holiday season and much luck and happiness in the New Year.

Most sincerely,

(555) 555-1234

INTERNET RESOURCES

These are really *Knock 'em Dead* Internet resources, with links to websites in twenty-two job search and career-management categories.

You'll find the big job banks; profession-specific sites for eighteen major industries; association, entry-level, executive, and minority sites; and more. You'll discover tools that help you find companies, executives, and lost colleagues, plus sites that help you choose new career directions or find a super-qualified professional resume writer or job or career coach.

To save time, you can come to the knockemdead.com website, where you can click on each of these resources and be connected directly—no more typing in endless URLs!

Association Sites

www.ipl.org
The Internet Public Library. Lots of great research services of potential use to your job search. This link takes you directly to an online directory of professional associations.

www.weddles.com
Peter Weddle's employment services site also offers a comprehensive online professional association directory.

Career and Job Coaches

www.knockemdead.com
Martin Yate, CPC, Executive Career Strategist
Email: *martin@knockemdead.com*
Typically works with C-level and C-level-bound professionals facing challenges in the areas of Job Search, Interviewing, and Career Strategy.

www.phoenixcareergroup.com
A private, by-invitation-only association of seasoned and credentialed coaches, of which I am a member. I know all the Phoenix consultants professionally, and I'm proud to know most of them personally. They're the finest you'll find.

www.certifiedcareercoaches.com
A website that features only certified career coaches.

www.certifiedresumewriters.com
A website that features only certified resume writers.

Career Assessments

www.assessment.com
A career choice test that matches your motivations against career directions. I've been using it for a number of years.

www.crgleader.com

www.careerplanning.about.com
Links to career planning and career choice tools. The first free career choice test listed wasn't very helpful, but the site has other good resources.

www.analyzemycareer.com
A well-organized and comprehensive career choice online testing site.

www.careerplanner.com
Affordable RIASEC-oriented career choice testing by an established online presence.

www.careertest.us

www.livecareer.com
Home page says it's free, and the free report is okay as far as it goes, which is not very far. To get a full report you will pay $25, and there are also premium options, but you don't know this until you have spent thirty minutes taking the test! Despite this sleight of hand, a good career choice test with comprehensive reports.

www.princetonreview.com
A $40 online test. This is a good solid test and the site is easy to navigate.

www.rockportinstitute.com
Excellent career choice tests for all ages. Although priced on a sliding scale dependent on income, they start at $1,500 for someone earning 40K a year or less.

www.self-directed-search.com
This is the famous SDS test developed by John Holland. An extremely well-regarded test, and at just $9.95 it's a great deal.

Career Choice and Management Sites

www.acinet.org
A site that offers career choice and advancement advice via testing for job seekers at all levels. Has good info on enhancing your professional credentials.

www.phoenixcareergroup.com
A premier site featuring deeply experienced and credentialed career counselors available for consultation on an hourly basis.

www.quintcareers.com
Career and job search advice.

www.rileyguide.com
Excellent site for job search and career-management advice. It's been around for years and is run by people who really care.

Career Transition
Military Transition

www.corporategray.com

www.taonline.com
Military transition assistance.

Other Transition

www.careertransition.org
For dancers once their joints go.

College and Entry-Level Job Sites

www.aleducation.com
Directories and links for colleges and graduate schools, test prep, financial aid, and job search advice.

www.aboutjobs.com
Links and leads for student jobs, internships, recent grads, expats, and adventure seekers.

www.aftercollege.com
Internships and co-ops, part-time and entry-level, PhDs and post-docs, teaching jobs, plus alumni links.

www.backdoorjobs.com
Short-term and part-time adventure and dream jobs.

www.blackcollegian.com
Premier site for black college students and recent graduates; help and sensible advice in areas of concern for the young professional.

www.campuscareercenter.com
Job search, career guidance, and advice on networking for transition into the professional world.

www.collegecentral.com
A networking site for graduates of small and medium-sized community colleges.

www.collegegrad.com
A comprehensive and well-thought-out site full of good information for the entry-level job seeker; probably the best in the entry-level field.

www.collegejobboard.com
A top job site for entry-level jobs; includes jobs in all fields.

www.collegejournal.com
Run by the *Wall Street Journal*, it's a savvy site for entry-level professionals, with lots of resources.

www.collegerecruiter.com
One of the highest-traffic sites for students and recent grads with up to three years' experience. Well-established and comprehensive job site.

www.entryleveljobs.net
It's been around since 1999, and it does have jobs posted, though much is out-of-date.

www.graduatingengineer.com
A site for graduating engineers and computer careers.

www.internshipprograms.com
A good site if you are looking for an internship.

www.snagajob.com
For part-time and hourly jobs.

College Placement and Alumni Networking

www.utexas.edu
Resource for locating college alumni groups.

Diversity Sites

http://janweb.icdi.wvu.edu
Job Accommodation Network: a portal site for people with disabilities.

www.twolingos.com
A site for bilingual jobs, in America and around the globe.

www.blackcollegian.com
Premier site for black college students and recent graduates; help and sensible advice in areas of concern for the young professional.

www.christianjobs.com
Full-featured employment website focusing on employment within the Christian community.

www.diversitylink.com
Job site serving women, minorities, and other diversity talent.

www.eop.com
The online presence of the oldest diversity recruitment publisher in America. For women, members of minority groups, and people with disabilities.

www.experienceworks.org
Training and employment services for mature workers, fifty-five and older.

www.imdiversity.com
Communities for African Americans, Asian Americans, Hispanic Americans, Native Americans, and women. No jobs or overt career advice, but lots of links for members of minority communities on issues that affect our lives.

www.latpro.com
The number one employment source for Spanish- and Portuguese-speaking professionals in North and South America The site can be viewed in English, Spanish, or Portuguese. Features both resume and job banks.

Executive Job Sites

www.netshare.com
Been around since before the Internet with tenured management; really understands and cares about the executive in transition. Job banks, resources, etc.

www.careers.wsj.com
Run by the *Wall Street Journal* with all the bells and whistles, this is an excellent executive transition site.

www.chiefmonster.com
Monster's site aimed at the executive area, though it's difficult to differentiate from the rest of the brand. Comprehensive job postings.

www.execunet.com
One of the top executive sites (along with Netshare, 6 Figure, and the WSJ site). Job banks and resources. Founder Dave Opton has been around a long time and runs a blog with interesting insights.

www.futurestep.com
Korn/Ferry is the search firm behind the site. You can put your resume in their database, which is not a bad idea.

www.spencerstuart.com
Executive site for eminent search firm Spencer Stuart. You can put your resume in their database.

www.theladders.com
Like pretty much all the executive sites, you pay for access. Good job board and aggressive marketing means this site has become a player in the space very quickly.

Finding Companies

www.flipdog.monster.com

www.corporateinformation.com
In addition to accessing an alphabetical listing of more than 20,000 companies, you can also research a country's industry or research a U.S. state. Also, if you register with the site, it will allow you to load the company profile. Within the address section, you will find a link to the company's home page.

www.zoominfo.com

www.goleads.com

www.google.com

www.infospace.com

www.searchbug.com

www.superpages.com

www.wetfeet.com

General Job Sites

www.flipdog.monster.com

www.hotjobs.yahoo.com

www.4jobs.com

www.americasjobbank.com

www.bestjobsusa.com

www.career.com

www.careerboard.com

www.careerbuilder.com

www.careerhunters.com

www.careermag.com

www.careers.org
Good one-stop site for job search resources.

www.careershop.com

www.careersite.com

www.employment911.com

www.employmentguide.com

www.employmentspot.com

www.jobcentral.com

www.job-hunt.org
Excellent site with sensible in-depth advice on job search and career-management issues.

www.job.com

www.jobbankusa.com

www.jobfind.com

www.localcareers.com

www.monster.com

www.nationjob.com

www.net-temps.com

www.quintcareers.com

Diversity Job-Seeker Career, Employment, Job Resources

www.snagajob.com

www.sologig.com

www.summerjobs.com

www.topusajobs.com

www.truecareers.com

www.vault.com

www.wetfeet.com

www.worklife.com

Job Posting Spiders

www.indeed.com

www.jobbankusa.com

www.jobsearchengine.com

International Sites

www.ukjobsnet.co.uk
UK Jobs Network: the easiest way to find vacancies throughout the United Kingdom.

www.4icj.com

www.careerone.com.au

www.eurojobs.com

www.gojobsite.co.uk

www.jobpilot.com

www.jobsbazaar.com

www.jobserve.com

www.jobstreet.com
Asia-Pacific's #1 job site.

www.monster.ca
Monster Canada

www.monster.co.uk
Monster UK: England's #1 job site.

www.overseasjobs.com

www.reed.co.uk

www.seek.com.au
Australia's #1 job site.

www.stepstone.com

www.topjobs.co.uk

www.totaljobs.com

www.workopolis.com
Canada's #1 job site.

Job Fairs

www.careerfairs.com
CareerFairs.com is the fastest one-stop Internet site for locating upcoming job fairs and employers. In some cases you can even find the specific positions you desire and the specific positions you are trying to fill.

www.cfg-inc.com
Career Fairs for all levels: Professional & General, Healthcare, Technical, Salary, Hourly, Entry to Senior Level.

www.skidmore.edu

Networking Sites

http://network.monster.com

http://socialsoftware.weblogsinc.com
This blog maintains a comprehensive listing of hundreds of networking sites. If you want to check out all your networking options, this is the place to start.

www.40plus.org
Chapter contact information.

www.alumni.net

www.distinctiveweb.com

www.zoominfo.com
Helps you find people and companies.

www.execunet.com
An extensive network of professionals with whom you can interact for advice, support, and even career enhancement through local networking meetings. To locate meetings near you (United States and the world), check under "Networking" on their website.

www.fiveoclockclub.com
National career counseling network.

www.rileyguide.com

www.ryze.com
Ryze helps people make connections and expand their networks. You can network to grow your business, build your career, and find a job. You can also join free networks related to your industry.

www.tribe.net

www.linkedin.com

Newspaper Sites

www.newsdirectory.com
Links to newspapers (global).

Profession-Specific Sites
Advertising, Public Relations, and Graphic Arts

www.adage.com

www.adweek.com
Adweek Online

www.amic.com
Advertising Media Internet Center

www.creativehotlist.com

Aerospace and Aviation

www.avcrew.com

www.avjobs.com

Agriculture and Horticulture

www.agcareers.com

www.fishingjobs.com

www.hortjobs.com

Broadcast, Communications, and Journalism

www.b-roll.net

www.cpb.org
Corporation for Public Broadcasting

www.crew-net.com

www.journalismjobs.com

www.telecomcareers.net

www.womcom.org
Association for Women in Communications
Online

Business, Finance, and Accounting

www.accounting.com

www.bankjobs.com

www.brokerhunter.com

www.businessfinancemag.com

www.careerbank.com

www.careerjournal.com

www.cfo.com

www.financialjobs.com

Communication Arts

www.prweek.com
PR Week

Education

www.aacc.nche.edu
American Association of Community Colleges

www.academic360.com

www.academiccareers.com

www.chronicle.com

www.higheredjobs.com

www.petersons.com

www.phds.org

www.teacherjobs.com

www.ujobbank.com

www.wihe.com
Women in Higher Education

Engineering

www.asme.org

www.chemindustry.com

www.engineeringcentral.com

www.engineeringjobs.com

www.engineerjobs.com

www.enr.com
Engineering News-Record Magazine

www.graduatingengineer.com

www.ieee.org

www.mepatwork.com

www.nsbe.org
National Society of Black Engineers

www.nspe.org
National Society of Professional Engineers

http://societyofwomenengineers.swe.org/

Entertainment, TV, and Radio

www.castingnet.com

www.entertainmentcareers.net

www.showbizjobs.com

www.themeparkjobs.com

www.tvandradiojobs.com

www.tvjobs.com

Health Care

http://allnurses.com

www.healthcaresource.com

www.healthjobsnationwide.com

www.hirehealth.com

www.jobscience.com

www.mdjobsite.com

www.medcareers.com

www.nurses123.com
Nurses can use this site to find nursing jobs across the United States.

www.nursetown.com

www.nursing-jobs.us
Nursing jobs in the United States.

www.nursingcenter.com

www.nurse.com

www.physemp.com

Human Resources

www.hrjobnet.com

www.hrworld.com

www.jobs4hr.com

www.shrm.org

IT and MIS

www.computerjobs.com

www.dice.com

www.gjc.org

www.mactalent.com

Legal

www.emplawyernet.com

www.ihirelegal.com

www.law.com

www.legalstaff.com

www.theblueline.com

Nonprofit

www.execsearches.com

www.idealist.org

www.naswdc.org

www.nonprofitcareer.com

www.opportunityknocks.org

Real Estate

www.realtor.org

Recruiter Sites

www.kellyservices.com

www.kornferry.com

www.manpower.com

www.napsweb.org
A job seeker can search the online directory by state, specialty, or by individual. Be sure to check out the headhunters who are designated CPCs—the few but the best.

www.randstad.com

www.recruitersonline.com

www.rileyguide.com

www.snelling.com

www.spherion.com

www.staffingtoday.net
Search the database by state, skills, and type of services you need (temporary/permanent/profession) and it will tell you about staffing services companies in your area.

www.therecruiternetwork.com

Reference Checking

www.allisontaylor.com

Researching Companies

www.bls.gov

www.fuld.com

www.newsdirectory.com

www.quintcareers.com
The Quintessential Directory of Company Career Centers, a guide to researching companies, industries, and countries.

www.thomasregister.com

www.vault.com
Company research

www.virtualpet.com
Teaches you how to learn about an industry or a specific company.

Resume Creation

Knockemdead.com
Email: *martin@knockemdead.com*

www.phoenixcareergroup.com

http://certifiedresumewriters.com

www.parw.com

Resume Distribution

www.resumemachine.com

Retail, Hospitality, and Customer Service

www.allretailjobs.com

www.chef2chef.net

www.chefjobsnetwork.com

www.coolworks.com

www.hcareers.com

www.leisurejobs.com

www.resortjobs.com

www.restaurantrecruit.com

www.supermarketnews.com

Salary Research

www.jobstar.org

www.salary.com

www.salaryexpert.com

Sales and Marketing

www.careermarketplace.com

www.jobs4sales.com

www.marketingjobs.com

www.marketingmanager.com

www.marketingpower.com

www.salesheads.com

www.salesjobs.com

Science, Chemistry, Physics, and Biology

www.biospace.com

www.bioview.com

www.eco.org

www.hirebio.com

www.medzilla.com

www.microbiologistjobs.com

www.pharmacyweek.com

Telecommuting

www.homeworkers.org

www.jobs-telecommuting.com

www.tjobs.com

For More Information

You can send me your comments and questions about any of the *Knock 'em Dead* books through my website at knockemdead.com, or by:

Emailing me at *martin@knockemdeud.com*

Or writing to me at:
Martin Yate
c/o Adams Media
57 Littlefield Street
Avon, MA 02322

The best of luck to you in your job search, and throughout your career!

GENERAL INDEX

INDEX OF SAMPLE LETTERS